THE STRUCTURE OF CHRISTIAN ETHICS

THE STRUCTURE
OF CHRISTIAN ETHICS

Joseph Sittler

Introduction by
Franklin Sherman

Westminster John Knox Press
Louisville, Kentucky

Introduction by Franklin Sherman © 1998 Westminster John Knox Press

Copyright 1958 by Louisiana State University Press

Library of Theological Ethics edition published by
Westminster John Knox Press 1998

This book is printed on acid-free paper that meets the American National Standards Institute Z39.48 standard. ∞

PRINTED IN THE UNITED STATES OF AMERICA

98 99 00 01 02 03 04 05 06 07 — 10 9 8 7 6 5 4 3 2 1

Library of Congress Cataloging-in-Publication Data

Sittler, Joseph.
    The structure of Christian ethics / Joseph Sittler ; introduction by
    Franklin Sherman.
            p.   cm. — (Library of theological ethics)
    Includes bibliographical references.
    ISBN 0-664-25763-1 (alk. paper)
    1. Christian ethics.   I. Title.   II. Series.
BJ1251.S43   1998
241—dc21   97-53205

CONTENTS

General Editors' Introduction   vii

Introduction by Franklin Sherman   ix

THE STRUCTURE OF CHRISTIAN ETHICS

Preface   1

  I   The Confusion in Contemporary Ethical Speech   3

 II   The Shape of the Engendering Deed   24

III   The Content of the Engendered Response   65

Notes to the Text   89

LIBRARY OF THEOLOGICAL ETHICS

General Editors' Introduction

The field of theological ethics possesses in its literature an abundant inheritance concerning religious convictions and the moral life, critical issues, methods, and moral problems. The Library of Theological Ethics is designed to present a selection of important texts that would otherwise be unavailable for scholarly purposes and classroom use. The series engages the question of what it means to think theologically and ethically. It is offered in the conviction that sustained dialogue with our predecessors serves the interests of responsible contemporary reflection. Our more immediate aim in offering it, however, is to enable scholars and teachers to make more extensive use of classic texts as they train new generations of theologians, ethicists, and ministers.

The volumes included in the Library comprise a variety of types. Some make available English-language texts and translations that have fallen out of print; others present new translations of texts previously unavailable in English. Still others offer anthologies or collections of significant statements about problems and themes of special importance. We hope that each volume will encourage contemporary theological ethicists to remain in conversation with the rich and diverse heritage of their discipline.

ROBIN W. LOVIN
DOUGLAS F. OTTATI
WILLIAM SCHWEIKER

INTRODUCTION

When this book was first published in 1958, Joseph Sittler had just completed his first year as professor of theology at the Divinity School of the University of Chicago. His career up to that point had been somewhat unusual. Like the great theologian and ethicist Reinhold Niebuhr, Sittler had never completed a Ph.D.; he cut his theological teeth in the task of preaching, serving for thirteen years as pastor of a Lutheran church in Cleveland, just as Niebuhr, his somewhat older contemporary, had done at a congregation in Detroit. In many respects, Sittler was self-taught, reading voraciously in many disciplines, especially in biblical studies, theology, and imaginative literature. In 1943, he was plucked out of the parish and appointed professor of systematic theology at Chicago Lutheran Theological Seminary in Maywood, Illinois, just as Niebuhr had gone from Detroit to Union Theological Seminary in New York. In 1957, Sittler was called to the University of Chicago, where he retired in 1973. Following that, he served until his death in 1987 as distinguished professor in residence at the Lutheran School of Theology at Chicago.

Joseph Sittler may be said to have been a "preacher's theologian," both in the sense that his own theological development was shaped by that pulpit experience and that his understanding of the theological task remained forever after that of assisting the church to articulate its historic faith in such a way as to address the full complexities of the modern age. Sittler, like Niebuhr, was a highly sought-after preacher to intellectuals; he was a favorite at college and university chapels all over the land. There was something of Tillich's "theology of correlation" in Sittler, an ability to penetrate into the nooks and crannies and nuances of contemporary self-understanding and bring forth from the theological tradition just what matched a particular issue or need. And there was an uncommon elegance in his language that allured the hearer or reader.

The title of this work, *The Structure of Christian Ethics,* might seem to promise more than it delivers, if by "structure" one means a fully developed scheme of logically interrelated categories and subcategories. Sittler, however, was well aware of what he was doing. In an earlier book, *The Doctrine of the Word,* Sittler had written of Martin Luther in words that might well be applied to himself. The question under discussion was whether Luther is or is not a systematic thinker. It all depends, Sittler wrote, on what one means by "systematic."

There is, to be sure, a sense of the term systematic thinker before which Luther would not qualify. If, that is, the connotation of system which is proper to propositional logic is made absolute, then Luther is not a systematic thinker. But we must decidedly reject any such presumption. There is a system proper to the dissection of the dead; and there is a system proper to the experience and description of the living. . . . A crystal has a system. But so does a living personality in the grip of a central certainty. If then by system one means that there is in a man's thought a central authority, a pervasive style, a way of bringing every theme and judgment and problem under the rays of the central illumination, then it must be said that history shows few men of comparable integration.[1]

"A living personality in the grip of a central certainty"—an apt description of Sittler himself. What was that central certainty for Sittler? He will speak for himself in the following pages, but we can venture to say that it was the dual certainty of the *reality of God* and the *primacy of grace.* "Grace" here means the unmerited mercy and invincible love of the true and living God, as made known in the biblical drama of creation and redemption, and as experienced in ever-surprising and wondrous ways in the midst of contemporary life. For Sittler, this meant a radically theocentric and radically Christocentric approach to Christian ethics, yet one that was open also to input from a wide range of secular thought. He refers, in the first chapter to follow, to the fact that we do Christian ethics not as isolated individuals, but as part of the great "cloud of witnesses," the saints and martyrs who have gone before. But he adds that there is a secular cloud of witnesses as well, in a stadium "as big as the world, as long as man's recorded history."[2]

From the beginning, Sittler thought on a grand scale, and it is not surprising that in the years immediately following the publication of this book, he moved on to the articulation of a "theology of nature," calling for a renewal of the "cosmic Christology" that had characterized an earlier period of Christian thought. He was influenced in this regard by his participation in the ecumenical movement, especially his encounter with Eastern Orthodoxy. Sittler's address to the New Delhi assembly of the World Council of Churches in 1961 served as a rallying cry for Christians all over the world to concern themselves with what came to be known as a "theology of the environment" or "ecological theology." For Sittler, it was all a part of the age-old problem of nature and grace: the salvific energies of grace must also be allowed to penetrate the world of nature. With Dietrich Bonhoeffer, he deplored all "thinking in terms of two spheres," whether in terms of the sacred vs. the secular, the personal vs. the social, or history vs. nature. "In him [Christ] all things hold together," Sittler was fond of quoting from Colossians.[3]

Does Sittler's approach to Christian ethics, as set forth in this book, amount to a form of situation ethics? *Prima facie,* the answer would seem to be yes. All that is needed, he says at one point, is "faith and the facts of life"—no middle principles, no ethical generalizations. The will of God, Sittler asserts, is made known "not as a general program given in advance but as an ever-changing and fluctuating obligation to the neighbor in the midst of history's life."[4] He interprets the New Testament in this same way. The Sermon on the Mount, and indeed all the teachings of Jesus, he declares, speak of a life of faith that "transcends every statutory solidification of duty, breaks out of all schematizations of the good."[5]

However, a closer inspection of his thought indicates that Sittler's viewpoint cannot be identified with some of the more simplistic versions of a situation ethic that were being promulgated at about that same time, such as that of Joseph Fletcher.[6] For one thing, Sittler strenuously resists the reduction of the "faith" side of the equation to the principle of love, which Fletcher makes all-determinative. Rather, Sittler pours into the notion of faith the whole content of the biblical revelation—not as a set of prescriptions but as a series of insights, incitements, demands, examples, and redemptive deeds that both call for our response and, by their own energies, shape the character of that response. The believer, for Sittler, is much more in the stance of reacting to a transformative encounter with the Holy than coolly reflecting on a range of choices. Second, regarding "facts," Sittler urges not just an immediate inspection of the situation, but employment of the full range of analytical and interpretive tools that are available, from whatever discipline. For him, the insights of the great poets, playwrights, and novelists were indispensable, transcending as they do the wisdom of any one person or any one generation. Thus, there is a greater complexity on both sides of this equation than might at first be apparent in the phrase "faith and the facts."

Although Sittler does not set forth a theory of natural law, he voices a kind of theological equivalent to it when he interprets the Ten Commandments as "a verbalization of the given structures of creation," and when he notes that "the quest for justice is a drive built into all human relationships."[7] Sittler recognizes that Christian ethics must push beyond a merely individualistic orientation: "Needs that are shaped by structures must be met by help that is also structured," he asserts, and he says of Christian love that "justice and technical competence are the hands it must work with."[8] Though Sittler did not go on to work out a comprehensive ethics of politics, or of the economic order, in subsequent years he did address a number of specific problems, usually in response to invitations to do so. These included such diverse topics as depersonalization in a mass society, trends in rural life, world peace and nuclear deterrence, issues in biomedical ethics, and aging, as well as his ongoing theme of ecology and the environment.[9]

While the title of this book is *The Structure of Christian Ethics,* perhaps Sittler's greatest contribution lies at the level of the shape and style of Christian ethics. "Shape" is one of Sittler's favorite terms—witness the chapter title "The Shape of the Engendering Deed" and his definition of the Christian life as "a reenactment from below on the part of men of the shape of the revelatory drama of God's holy will in Jesus Christ."[10] Sittler sometimes referred to this shape as "the parabola of grace," based on the Pauline depiction in Philippians 2 of the self-emptying incarnation of the logos and the divine identification with the depths of human life. The downward swoop of incarnation and crucifixion is followed by the upward swoop of resurrection, and with it the reaffirmation of all that is noble and the will-toward-healing of all that is ignoble in human life. This is the shape of God's deed, and at the same time the shape of the Christian's response, who enters fully into both life's joys and sufferings (incarnation/crucifixion) and serves as a vehicle of resurrection grace. Again, Sittler found a kindred spirit in Dietrich Bonhoeffer, who in his *Ethics* speaks in remarkably similar terms of Christian ethics as "conformation with Christ."[11]

Sittler was a poet at heart; language meant a great deal to him in ethical discourse. We can be grateful for the eloquence of his utterances, which themselves have an engendering and empowering quality. But he meant something more than this by "style." Perhaps it is close to "stance," in the sense of the whole attitude that one takes toward a subject, or the fundamental bearing of the ethical actor, preceding and yet also accompanying the ethical action. One of Sittler's favorite quotations was a remarkable statement by the nuclear physicist J. Robert Oppenheimer that Sittler found in a symposium on "The Limits of Language." In a section titled "A Definition of Style," Oppenheimer writes:

> The problem of doing justice to the implicit, the imponderable, and the unknown is of course not unique to politics. It is always with us in science, it is with us in the most trivial of personal affairs and it is one of the great problems of writing and of all forms of art. The means by which it is solved is sometimes called style. It is style which complements affirmation with limitation and with humility; it is style which makes it possible to act effectively, but not absolutely; it is style which, in the domain of foreign policy, enables us to find a harmony between the pursuit of ends essential to us and the regard for the views, the sensibilities, the aspirations of those to whom the problem may appear in another light; it is style which is the deference that action pays to uncertainty; it is above all style through which power defers to reason.[12]

This is the style in which Joseph Sittler wanted us to do ethics: with a continual awareness of "the implicit, the imponderable, and the unknown," and yet also with the confidence that if we endeavor, in Lincoln's words, "to do the right, as God gives us to see the right," our inherently ambiguous actions will be caught up into the grandeur of God's purposes.

FRANKLIN SHERMAN

NOTES

1. Joseph Sittler, *The Doctrine of the Word* (Philadelphia: Muhlenberg Press, 1948), 3f. The use of noninclusive terms such as "man" and "men" in this and other quotations from Sittler is, of course, due to their date of origin.

2. Joseph Sittler, *The Structure of Christian Ethics* (Louisville, Ky.: Westminster John Knox Press, 1998), 20.

3. Colossians 1:17. Cf. Dietrich Bonhoeffer, *Ethics,* ed. Eberhard Bethge (New York: Macmillan Co., 1955; latest revised edition, New York: Simon and Schuster, 1995).

4. Sittler, *The Structure of Christian Ethics,* 73.

5. Ibid., 48.

6. Joseph Fletcher, *Situation Ethics: The New Morality* (Louisville, Ky.: Westminster John Knox Press, 1997).

7. Sittler, *The Structure of Christian Ethics,* 70, 76.

8. Ibid., 75, 77.

9. Much of this remained unpublished, but for some published examples see the essay "Christian Theology and the Environment" in Sittler, *Essays on Nature and Grace* (Philadelphia: Fortress Press, 1972) and the sections "Moral Discourse in a Nuclear Age" and "Aging: A Summing Up and a Letting Go" in Sittler, *Gravity and Grace: Reflections and Provocations,* a collection of his occasional writings edited by Linda-Marie Delloff (Minneapolis: Augsburg, 1986). Unpublished materials are held in the Sittler Archive at the Lutheran School of Theology at Chicago.

10. Sittler, *The Structure of Christian Ethics,* 36.

11. Bonhoeffer, op. cit. See the section titled "Ethics as Formation."

12. W. Walker Gibson, ed., *The Limits of Language* (New York: Hill & Wang, 1962), 50f.

THE STRUCTURE OF CHRISTIAN ETHICS

PREFACE

The material here presented was delivered at The Rice Institute, Houston, Texas, as a series of Rockwell Lectures. I am grateful both for the invitation to prepare these lectures, and for the thoughtful courtesy of many members of the faculty and administration of the Institute during my days in Houston.

The earliest occasion to set down an argument for the structure of Christian ethics was provided by a directive of my own Church that a Commission prepare a rather full statement for the guidance of our people as, in the midst of confusing and deepening ethical problems, they look for a solid center from which to learn what they ought to do. Large sections of my contribution to that study, which appeared in the summer of 1957 under the title *Christian Social Responsibility* (Philadelphia: Muhlenberg Press), are reproduced here by permission of the publisher.

JOSEPH SITTLER

The University of Chicago
May, 1958

The Confusion in Contemporary
Ethical Speech

THE effort in this first lecture is descriptive. The
second and third lectures are a constructive effort
to indicate the ground and the main lines of development of characteristically biblical ethics. And inas-
much as the assertions there advanced will cut across
what is commonly assumed to be a proper way to
derive ethical decisions from the Bible, they will
commend themselves to our attention to the extent
that they are shown to arise with naturalness, integrity, and clarity from the biblical material. The
substance of this first lecture will be elaborated under
three topics.

The Organic Nature of Biblical Speech

When a man of the twentieth century, divesting
himself of the ways of thought normal to his time
and place, wanders back into the speech-world and
thought-world of the Bible he finds himself in a
strange and puzzling land. The very structural elements of his common assumptions are there either
gently laid aside in what he listens to, or are simply
ignored. God, man, nature—these are the large fields
of concern and enquiry now, as they have always
been. But what strikes the reader of the Bible with

almost the force of a palpable blow is the fact that these categories—among us separated for purposes of enquiry and description—are in the Bible but aspects of a single actuality, God himself. Our speech is specialized in order to achieve precision in the description of our world as it presents itself to us under a multitude of forms. The biblical speech is thoroughly organic.

God is the Creator. He is the fountain of life from whose eternal livingness all things are brought forth. As the up-arching lines of an exploding rocket describe parabolic arcs of light against the darkness, so does the Bible speak of all the elements, forms, forces, in the world. "The earth is the Lord's and the fulness thereof." God is not identified with the world, for he *made* it; but God is not separate from his world, either. For *He* made it. This God is never defined, his existence proved, or his nature elaborated in rational categories. God simply *is* what God manifestly does. When, for instance, the man of the Old Testament speaks about God he does not introduce his speech with an exhibition of a general truth, that there is a God, or by appeal to generalities of truth, goodness, or power in relation to which God is certified and accredited. He simply assumes that God, whose nature, will, and purpose has been made clear in his people's history, is alive, demanding and loving —and that men's lives can have no conceivable mean-

4

ing or goodness save in obedient hearing and serving. What God is, that is to say, is an organic function of what God does.

The biblical speech about man has the same organic character. His existence is a subsistence. Man-in-himself is an inconceivable idea. Man *has* his existence by the Word of God. *Who* he is is organic with *whence* he is. How he should live is continuous with *where* he is—under God. If we did not so assiduously address to the first chapter of Genesis questions which are there neither raised nor answered, we should long since have heard them for what they are —a hymn to God the Creator. The fact that God made Eve, so sufficiently and delightfully different as to secure the propogation of the race, is not by any means the primary point. That he made her *at all* suggests the preliminary truth—that a solitary person is no person. Man, that is to say, is not only constituted in, by, and for organic relation to God who made him, but also for organic relation to other persons.

This radical vocabulary of relatedness characterizes every primary term of the Bible. Man is made in the image of God. He cannot become what he is if he ignores, denies, defies his structural God-relationship. And sin, too, is an organic term, for it designates a fractured relationship. God is life. Man has his life from God. If this Gift-Source of his life is repudi-

5

ated, man no longer has life. He is then dead—whether the amenities of the funeral have taken place or not. That is precisely what is said in the statement that the wages, or outcome, of sin is death. The New Testament speech of our Lord presupposes this organic understanding. Man's life is a branch of a trunk of life and it flowers when the connection is there.

And the term *righteousness*—by us so commonly indicative of moral probity, avoidance of glaring and dramatic wrongdoing—is in the Bible a term that indicates the state of a man's God-relationship. The Hebrew term translated *righteousness* has exactly this meaning. It means to be right, vitally related to one's source, to live in such a way as to affirm and celebrate the God from whom one has his life. That is why, in the Bible, men are called to be righteous only on the ground that God is righteous. Men are not called to an ideal, or threatened with failure to match an elevated standard of abstract goodness. They are called rather to be what they are, live their true life, realize their being in their existence, and work out their relationships on earth in organic continuity with their relationship to the Creator.

The organic terms with which the Bible speaks of God and man inform also the biblical speech about nature. I am not, at the moment, weighing the adequacy of this speech for all aspects of natural science

6

investigation, although the introduction of theological ideas into scientific discourse is not so obviously ridiculous as it appeared some decades ago. The present effort is to achieve a vivid appreciation of a type of discourse characteristic of the Bible, and re-establish the category of the organic as the natural climate in which biblical terms must be heard and understood.

When, then, the Bible speaks of nature it does not introduce an entity for the description of which a new set of terms has to be invented. God made the world as he made man—by his Word. The life of nature is a given life. The entities, forms, processes of the natural world are, for the biblical writer, facts of wonder, but not of ultimate mystery. Typical of this organic continuity between God and nature is the lyrical celebration in the 104th Psalm of the inter-relatedness of the life of nature. Just as God placed his creature, man, in a garden and commanded him to " tend " it, so the world of nature—God's other creation—is spoken of as man's context in which is celebrated the same orchestration of relatedness. We are indeed dull of heart if we permit the naiveté of the lyricism to conceal from us the theology of the cosmos that sings through this Psalm. The light is God's garment, the heavens a cosmic curtain, the clouds the chariots of God, the wind and the thunder his voice. The springs, the birds, the growing grass, the grazing cattle—and consuming man—are all tied together in the bundle of Holy care.

> He causeth the grass to grow for the cattle; and herb for the service of man; That he may bring forth food out of the earth, and wine that maketh glad the heart of man; and oil to make his face to shine, and bread that strengtheneth man's heart. (Ps. 104:14)

This poem of interdependence is, however, all introductory to the consummate intention: that the million strands of dependency might illumine and confirm the shining cord of absolute dependency upon which the whole nexus hangs, through which its given life flows as a current from the Power-Source of the Holy.

> These all wait upon Thee . . . . Thou sendest forth Thy Spirit, they are created; . . . Thou hidest Thy face, they are troubled: Thou takest away their breath, they die, and return to their dust. (Ps. 104:27, 30, 29)

The Transformation of Biblical Speech in the Thought of the Church

When, to the first generation following the life of Jesus, a member of the community of faith addressed in practical terms the sodden moral life of his generation, there can still be heard through his language

8

the authentic power of the Bible's organic speech. To the Church in Rome Paul says, " I appeal to you therefore, brethren by the mercies of God, to present your bodies as a living sacrifice, holy and acceptable to God, which is your spiritual worship."

The force of the appeal rests here, not upon an abstract ethical ideal, nor upon any appeal to the self-destruction implicit in egocentricity and immorality, but as the " therefore " clearly indicates, upon a prior action of God whose force must either be confirmed and obeyed in a totally new " presentation of the body " (that is, a complete new orientation of the entire personality) or utterly rejected. Another kind of logic than that required by a cause and effect understanding of life is at work here. Side by side with the necessities of cause and effect (whose logic, in our western mental history is expressed in space terms) there is another kind of necessity. It is the inner logic of the living, the organic, the destiny-bound. And *its* logic is expressed in time terms. Entrance into the world of the second kind of discourse is simply not possible through the kind of cognition proper to the first. Where, that is to say, we read the New Testament story of the encounter of the life of God with the life of man in terms of the causality principle taken over from natural science, we not only do *not* confront and receive the ethical vitality of the New Testament message, but we positively

9

distort it. For we then impose upon a living nexus of organic powers and responses the forms of our own sensibility. The immediacies of biblical-ethical command are not communicable in the causalities of propositional speech; the vital unfolding into a new-being which is presaged by Paul's ". . . be ye transformed by the renewing of your minds . . ." is not communicable except in connection with the picture of God which grounds it—and which Paul assumes when he introduces his Apostolic counsel with the phrases, " Well, then . . . for this cause . . . therefore, brethren . . . . Because God, who is rich in mercy," and so on.

While, to be sure, this transposition of the organic vitality of Biblical speech into the abstract, intellectualized and propositional form of Western theology has been illustrated here by ethically loaded statements, the *process* was nonetheless general. And so pervasive has this process been that a great historian of Christian thought once described the entire body of Western church dogma as an " acute Hellenization of Christianity." Space does not allow a detailed examination of even the main lines of this process, but evidences of the transformative power of it can be indicated. The organic structure of the New Testament doctrine of the Church has, for most Protestant believers, become so drained of its proper character that the discovery of the living and relational language of the New Testament, due in part to the encounter and studies encouraged by the Ecumenical Movement, come as a positive shock. The Church is not, in the New Testament, a sociological quantum discoverable or mensurable by categories available anywhere in man's experience. The Church is the fellowship of the faithful which is created and bound together, *not* by men's mutual perception of a common faith in themselves, or religion, or even in God, but by the faithfulness of God become concrete in a body. This body was the actual historical appearing of a Man; and the Church, the body of Christ, is the organic household of the "members" of the body. Before the Church is the company of them that love God, it is the communion of them who acknowledge, and in that acknowledgment have their lives given a new center in One who loved them. The passive verb dominates the New Testament story! I love because I am loved; I know because I am known; I am of the Church, the body of Christ, because this body became my body; I can and must forgive because I have been forgiven; I can speak because I have been spoken to.

The confusion let loose in contemporary ethical discourse by the failure to relate ethical commands organically to the ethical Commander, reveals itself most fully in what one might call the ethics-of-the-end-of-the-sentence! The ethical teaching of Jesus, for instance, is commonly excised from his entire address to man, in word and in deed; and an effort is made to ask after the meaning and applicability of the end of a sentence, the first part of which we impatiently dismiss as having only local or occasional significance for the speaker and his first century hearers. This practice is rather like dropping in on a performance of a Bach fugue in time to hear the last page. The organic content of Jesus' address to men was not composed of highly personal epigrams consensed from the most elegant moral idealism ever envisioned by man in his quest for the good. This content was constituted, rather, by a lived-out and heroically obedient God-relationship in the fire of which all things are what they are by virtue of the Creator, all decisions are crucial in virtue of their witness to his primacy and glory, all events interpreted in terms of their transparency, recalcitrancy, or service to God's Kingly rule.

The Instrumental Evaluation of Ethics

There are evidences that our modern American enthusiasm for that aspect of Christian faith which is called *ethics* includes a covert form of idolatry—the more perilous because so disguised. There is a relation between the knowledge of God and the achievement and maintenance of human order; but God does not commonly make himself available to men who seek him primarily to achieve and maintain order. If God is sought in order to integrate the personality, the actual God is not God but the integrated personality. And when men are urged to renovate their religious values in order that the Republic may be the more firmly glued together, this covert idolatry reaches a peculiarly pernicious and untruthful pitch. There is a relation between a people who are blessed because their God is the Lord, but one does not find it recorded that God the Lord consents to be compounded into political glue.

It is instructive to examine the way the name of God, and appeals to his help, are introduced into the public political utterances of our leading politicos. The situation is described; some elements in it are announced as gratifying, others as deplorable. A vigorous program is then outlined, the hardship its execution will work upon our tax rate is confronted, and justified. And, finally, having figured out and announced what our rôle is, or ought to be, and what at the moment must be done, the entire structure of analysis and purpose is immersed in the tub of the waiting blessing of God. The performance concludes with the obvious assumption that from such commendable purposes God would not be so churlish as to withhold his effective assistance.

This understanding of Christian ethics—as a lubricant for the adjustment of the personality, and as an adhesive for public policy—does violence to the reality of both Christianity and politics. It does violence to Christianity because it makes the Holy a disposable object to be manipulated for mortal purposes; it does violence to political order because it tempts to such an identification of our purposes with the purposes of God as to engender both arrogance and insensitivity.

Nowhere, perhaps, in the recorded utterances of our English speaking men of affairs is there reflected so clearly as in President Lincoln's Second Inaugural Address the unfathomable mystery of the relationship between the purposes of God and the ethical crusades of men.

> Both (men of the North and of the South) read the same Bible, and pray to the same God; and each invokes his aid against the other . . . . The prayers of both could not be answered—that of neither has been answered fully.
> The Almighty has his own purposes.

It is necessary now to gather up the argument of this introductory lecture. The effort has been to expose the confusion in contemporary discourse about Christian ethics by way of an analysis of what seem to be three of its constituents. They are these: first, a failure to remain sensitive to the organic character of the biblical speech about God, man, and nature in such a way as to be aware that ethics is a function of faith, that ethics is faith-doing, that the living continuity between man-in-God and man-among-men is basic to the perception of the biblical revelation; second, the transposition of organic biblical unity of faith and life into categories of a cause and effect structure in Christian ethical systems, with the result that the living unity of faithful obedience has dwindled into abstract counsels, duties, obligations; and, third, that most religious form of idolatry whereby the Holy is understood from the point of view of, made malleable by, and turned into an instrument of, men's autonomous purposes.

In Oswald Spengler's *Decline of the West* is so concise and brilliant an analogy of this confusion-begetting process that I give here the entire paragraph:

> In a rock-stratum are embedded crystals of a mineral. Clefts and cracks occur, water filters in, and the crystals are gradually washed out so that in due course only their hollow mould remains. Then come volcanic outbursts which explode the mountain; molten masses pour in, stiffen, and crystallize out in their turn. But these are not free to do so in their own special forms. They must fill up the space that they find available. Thus there are distorted forms, crystals whose inner structure contradicts their shape, stones of one kind presenting the appear-

ance of stones of another kind. The minerolo-
gists call this phenomenon *Pseudomorphosis*.[1]

In addition to the confusion-begetting factors elaborated above there is something other and something
more that has to be said. It lies deeper down and
further back; and the substance of it, while not for-
mally a part of the foregoing analysis cannot be ignored. To ignore it would be to fail to say what has
to be said if justice is to be done to the deepest levels
where one becomes aware of ethical questions, and is
motivated to ponder them.

One does not study the Bible, teach Christian theology, live out his life, in a vacuum—even a vacuum
modified by persons who share his concern, belong
to the church, are deferential to the Christian tradition. My own career as a preacher and a teacher
of the Christian faith has been and continues to be
fulfilled in the company of as various, uninhibited,
sometimes ribald, always candid talkers as a continuous affection for literature can supply. The New
Testament letter to the Hebrews speaks of the man
of faith bearing witness to it in this world like an
athlete on a playing field of a great stadium ringed
round with a " mighty cloud of witnesses." While I,
too, work as a teacher in that stadium of the Christian centuries wherein I am instructed, consoled, and
heartened by the yet-living presences of the saints, I

16

am also a citizen of the world of my human brothers. There *they* sit, too, the living and the dead. They cheer and jeer, commend and criticize, throw their hats in derision and despair—and jarringly continue to talk back!

As one tries to penetrate to the structure and content of Christian ethics he cannot shut these people up, or think and act as if they were not there. They are a noisy and insistent lot. How richly our literature sparkles with works in which these men and women have made articulate their perception of the gap between man's wild, unsystematic self and the ordered thoughts, principles, institutions through which he wills to be known and honored! This literature of perception and enquiry includes ways of speaking so different and names so seemingly unrelated as Boccaccio, Cervantes, Montaigne, Blake, Hardy, Jane Austen, Hawthorne, Melville, Eliot, Cummings, Shaw, and Tennessee Williams.

What this strange crowd has in common is simply that they have each seen something wrong, or pathetic, or humorous with the way the Christian story gets itself realized in the theatre of our common human experience. The core of the story, its central affirmations, is not commonly the target of their attack or their customary sardonic comment. The story says that God has acted for man's healing, that this action became concrete in an Incarnation, that in consequence human life has available a new relation to God, a new light for seeing, a new fact and center for thinking, a new ground for forgiving and loving, a new context for acting in this world. A surprising number of this company have got that pretty straight.

The burden of the literary comment is rather in the area *between* God's action and the " Christian " behavior of the human beings supposedly determined by it. The integral character of the action seems to get lost or distorted, its organic wholeness fragmented into morsels of accredited mores. And because the authority and solemnity of the action is so vast, the failure, brokenness, hypocrisy, and humorless insensitivity of the human response provide so rich a fare for the artist as critic. It is this hiatus between the transcendent authority and origination of the ethical pattern and an all too earthly performance (often conjoined with pontifical refusal to admit as much) which is the substance of the literary commentary. *That* is what Boccaccio is documenting; Montaigne quietly smiling about; Blake bitter about. Hardy unfolds the pathetic, mad occasionalism of common incidents in such a way as to construct an attack upon the Christian assumption that God cares at all about human lives; Shaw slashes away at the ambiguities hidden away under the cover of men's moral pretensions.

That men do not perform as they profess, that

they do not live up to their announced belief—this is old and obvious stuff, and there is a sufficient literature of admonition on the subject. But the smile, or the anger, or the sardonic twist in the literature here recalled delivers a quite different and a deeper judgment. It's as if these writers suspected that some basic and horrible *misunderstanding* had occurred between God the Speaker and man the hearer. Soren Kierkegaard called it an "acoustical illusion" whereby man accredits his acoustical echo with original authority! Men set about being "ethical" under the impact and continuing power of the Gospel, within the tutorial structure of the Church, and in the light of those ordered presentations of obligation called Moral Theology. And on the way they burn witches; fight wars out of mixed purposes which they persuade themselves are not mixed at all; use venerable and holy names to designate institutions and practices which they dare not criticize, lest they threaten worldly securities; pose, posture, lie, and generally pervert the organic integrity of the life of faith.

All of this is but a way of saying that efforts to gain the truth about the Christian ethical life must operate in the two stadia of our existence as Christian men. There is the "mighty cloud of witnesses" who ensconce our unfolding days in their embattled song of faith, their firm hymn of confession and testimony to the salvatory power of God in Jesus Christ. And there is that other stadium, as big as the world, as long as man's recorded history, incessantly talking back to

>... the burthen of the mystery,
>... the heavy and the weary weight
>Of all this unintelligible world. . . .

And, between delight and despair, creating forms in language, in visual arts, and in music in which, as Mr. Peter Viereck puts it, man scrawls across his fluctuant scene the defiant " Kilroy was here! "

It is an act of almost humane piety which moves me to record here how great is the debt owed by the teacher of ethics to the company of his fellows who attend his soberer efforts with their disconcerting observations. In my own experience Miss Jane Austen has been a particularly infuriating person! Just when her age, in her tight little island, was convinced that most human problems if not in the bag were on the way to it—everything ordered, civilized, proportional—she turned loose her light, unengaged, girlish, and terribly penetrating laughter upon the whole performance! She exposed, not with a Shavian club or Trollope's broad, humorous gesture, but with genteel pricks of a knitting needle, as it were, the absurd incongruities between form and fact, the dear delusions so sweetly anesthetic to a conventional society.

This amazing spinster is an instance of the fundamentally ethical nature of the craft of the artist. The task of the artist, as artist, is not to declare directly the Gospel of God; it is rather to speak the truth about the life of man, to let real cats out of phoney bags. That is what Stendal does in the *Red and the Black*, Dostoevskii in *The Brothers Karamazov*, and Tennessee Williams in *Cat on a Hot Tin Roof*. These remind all ordered placidity that living truth is tougher than composure, that man has a gallant, godly habit of shattering, on solider ground again to build—that cracked conclusions are the casualties of his human career.

I had not been driven so deeply into the center of the ethical teaching of Jesus, had I in professorial retreat kept at arm's length this company of man's confessors. Nor would I so surely feel, as I do, that the Christian Gospel is both profounder in its analysis of the ambiguous ethical self, and alone adequate to what this analysis discloses, had I not had my ethical perceptions made articulate in the labors of the artist.

There is, for an example, Herman Melville. *Redburn* is an account in which the problem of the good and the evil, and all the disguises of both, is recorded in a young man's growing up in the wide world of men. *Moby Dick* is a wild novel in which the problem is stated with a symbolical clarity unmatched in American literature. But long after the maniacal fury of Moby Dick, when Melville in the autumnal calm of his last months groped toward an answer and felt the shape of it to be the ancient form of a cross, and a crucified man—*Billy Budd* was written, and laid away in a drawer.

W. H. Auden, in his short poem, *Herman Melville*, has celebrated the quiet, inward drama of Melville's movement toward maturity, and I close this first lecture with some lines from it.

> Towards the end he sailed into an extraordinary
>   mildness . . . .

> Goodness existed: that was the new knowledge
> His terror had to blow itself quite out
> To let him see it . . . .

> Evil is unspectacular and always human,
> And shares our bed and eats at our own table,
> And we are introduced to Goodness every day,
> Even in drawing-rooms among a crowd of faults;
> He has a name like Billy and is almost perfect
> But wears a stammer like a decoration:
> And every time they meet the same thing has to
>   happen;
> It is the Evil that is helpless like a lover
> And has to pick a quarrel and succeeds,
> And both are openly destroyed before our eyes . . . .

> And all the stars above him sang as in his childhood
> " All, all is vanity," but it was not the same;
> For now the words descended like the calm of
>   mountains—

—Nathaniel had been shy because his love was
  selfish—
But now he cried in exultation and surrender
" The Godhead is broken like bread. We are the
  pieces."
And sat down at his desk and wrote a story.[2]

The Shape of the Engendering Deed

A BRIEF look at the three terms of the title of this lecture, against the concepts of organism and morphology set forth in the first lecture, will advance us quickly and clearly into its substance. The term *shape* is used here to recall and to assert: to recall the organic and total nature of the biblical way of speaking about God and man; to assert that the same type of discourse must be continued into the field of ethics if confusion is to be avoided.

The term *deed* is used in order to bring into focus that understanding of the Scriptures which accepts them as records and witnesses to what the living God has actually done in creation, redemption, and sanctification. The reception of this deed in man's mental and moral career has, to be sure, to be related to general terms in man's vocabulary of high abstraction. And for that reason it is necessary and proper to speak of the idea of God, the structure of the God-concept, the philosophy of religion, the psychology of faith, the cultic character of the form of the Church. Each of these terms designates a discipline, some quite new, others very old, in which data and methods proper to these fields of enquiry are employed in an effort to understand the content of the specifically biblical terms, and evaluate their meaning. But the term *deed of God* is calculatedly chosen to invite the mind to ponder the particularity of the biblical speech so that the intrinsically specific quality of its referents may be grasped and honored.

The term *engendering* is used to assert that the organic relationship between God and man structured into existence in creation, incarnated into absolute involvement in redemption, persists and inwardly determines the realm of sanctification, that is, the field of Christian ethics. God's deed does not simply call, or present a pattern in front of, or evoke, or demonstrate. It *engenders*; that is, it brings into existence lives bred by its originative character. Only terms which denote a quasi-biological-organic relationship are adequate to elaborate in terms of ethics what is declared of the reality of the Christian God in his work for man's situation.

It was the perception of the necessity that all Christian speech begin with what God does and gives that moved a towering Christian scholar to make the astonishingly simple and profound statement that to be a Christian is to accept what God gives.

What God gives is the theme of the Bible. This going out from Himself in creative and redemptive action toward men is, within the Bible itself, the basic meaning of the *Word of God*. " By the Word of the Lord were the heavens made "; " The Word became flesh and dwelt among us." The Scriptures are called Word of God because they are a literature in which alone this action of the Word of God is recorded, witnessed to, and—in the hearing of the message there contained—continued. It is not strange, therefore, that the form of the Scriptures should be a drama. For drama is the form appropriate for the enunciation of movement, action, doing.

If, then, the Scriptures are a literature which depicts the action of God, is it possible so to peer into the remembered and recorded action in such a way as to evoke from among the multitudinous events, responses, utterances, the massive shape of the entire complex? It is in the confidence that this is possible that I have entitled this lecture " The Shape of the Engendering Deed."

The Bible tells man who he is and how he has gotten into his predicament. To tell him this is the intention of the stories of creation, rebellion, fall. The very dramatic character of these accounts indicates that they are God's revelation about himself, about man, nature, the ground of human community —all of these separately and in their relationship. A drama is never a slice out of life content to be only that. It is a section which reveals, like the tissue section under the eye of the pathologist, the condition of the entire organism. What is revealed in this biblical section of the situation far transcends the ancient persons, places, and events which are its

26

occasion. The Creator and his creature, God-will and man-will, love creative of fellowship and lust breeding estrangement, man in the garden of his peace and man self-evicted into the relationship to nature which now along with man "groans in travail, waiting . . . ." These are the mighty dramatic themes which swirl in a multitude of tender and terrible shapes through the record of God's ancient people.

Books of prophecy, books of passionate and contemplative song, books of history and chronicle, all, if we listen for the motif that grounds their wonderful variety, sing out the theme of holy conflict: God-will and man-will. Not in abstract form or fictionalized persons, but richly rooted in human life and history, in nature, and in social life, the conflict unfolds the undeviating self-giving of God and the career of the gift among men. Old Testament history has a grand pattern; it is the weary rhythm of rebellion, repentance, and return; and over and over again the rhythm repeats itself. In the book of the Judges the writer seems actually to have managed his historical materials to accent the repetitive monotony of this pattern. Old Testament song and literature of devotion swings always and with opulent variation about the two poles: God's relentless gift of himself in steadfast love and man's desperate shadow-flight from love's undismissible grounding of his life. Old Testament prophecy, attached to anecdotal history at a thousand points, and made articulate in many voices and many keys, has nevertheless a simple pattern. The figure of the prophet is the unsilenceable recollection of man's structurally given existence before God; and the up-welling voice of the prophet, through crusts of assumed independence and national self-sufficiency, through proudly contrived historical securities and subtly imagined individual safety, is the grave, recalling voice of God. The " whither shall I flee " of the individual singer has its large prophetic counterpart in the word addressed to the whole people, " I have called thee by thy name, thou art mine."

In the Old Testament drama God's love and mercy are never presented as simply God's feeling about apostate man. Love and mercy are rather the forms in which God's resolute will-to-restoration presses upon man. The love of God is a loving will; and the outstretched arm of the Eternal has many aspects. It is both beckoning and judging; but it is always there—the Creator of the drama, the Holy One with whom man has inescapably to do. As the Old Testament literature moves on toward its close the conflict tightens in both divine and mortal terms. In divine terms the assault of God tightens; hope is condensed from a holy nation to a remnant, and finally to the form of a Servant of the Lord. In mortal terms, the drama of alienation depicts man, ingenious in evasion and flight and self-deception, able at the last only to cry, " Oh, that thou wouldst rend the heavens, that thou wouldst come down."

Only against this background can one understand why the Evangelists of the New Testament surround the nativity of Jesus Christ with heavenly messengers and choirs, poetic condensations of the hope of Israel, the Virgin's lyrical song of acceptance. Everything seems to stand still and all things are bathed in luminous light when the new deed of God occurs in Jesus Christ. It is not in fact a strange deed if beheld from above. For God's undeviating will-to-restoration but assumes here a decisive tactic of mortal involvement. But seen from below this tactic is unique, utterly singular. For here, claim the Scriptures, is God himself in salvatory, that is, restorative action at the point and at the level of the original rupture. When the Fourth Gospel declares that the Word became flesh and dwelt among us, the new deed of God in Christ is declared in clearest terms; the involvement of the Holy Will can come to no closer engagement than this: *flesh* which is what I am, *among us* which is where I am!

Is it possible to speak of the career of Jesus of Nazareth in such a way as responsibly to include in a simple pattern the total self-giving of God, which Jesus himself, the apostles, and the faith of the Church, have declared to be the meaning of the total deed? The Scriptures themselves declare this to be possible; and, indeed, the earliest declarations of the community of faith achieve this simplicity. The parables of the Kingdom turn about a common center: God in a fresh and decisive way is at work in His world. The miracle-stories are dramatic signs which underline the impact of this liberating action of God. And the teaching of Jesus which accompanies these " signs " has its center in his announcement that a news event no less astonishing than the creation of the Cosmos has occurred. Its occurrence has brought Him with it, and thus made itself available to men on earth. The Gospels present the intention and work of Jesus in terms of an actual power-conflict in which the will of God does desperate battle with the tyrants of life that hold man in a dungeon of estrangement, cut off from his proper life, his proper ground. What these terms point to is an action of God in Jesus Christ, whereby everything that operates to separate God and man has, from God's side and by the gracious assault of his deed in Christ, been overcome.

It is within the orbit of this gracious and aggressive overcoming activity of God that the death and resurrection of Jesus is to be understood. Outside that orbit, understood only from below, that death engenders not peace but despair, not joy but bitterness. So viewed it constitutes an appalling confirmation of ultimate futility. But when understood from above, as the supreme function of God's will-to-restoration ("God was in Christ, reconciling the world unto Himself")—the death of Christ is seen as the triumphant work of restoration operative precisely at the point of desolation. In the deed of Christ on Calvary there takes place the absolute involvement of God with the absolute tragedy of man. "Herein is love, not that we love God, but that he loved us."

If the drama of restoration were to end at this point, it would accomplish no restoration. To be joined in my cell-of-dying by no other than God himself would but magnify the private pathos of mutability to the dimensions of cosmic tragedy.

"But God hath raised him up!" The meaning of that declaration of the primitive Christian community is by no means exhausted in the episode of the resurrection. The resurrection is, to be sure, the center to which such an assertion points, but the circumference of it embraces the entire God-man relationship for all time. This statement declares that the entire movement of God's loving will-to-restoration, having taken the form of the Christ-servant and having swept down into the nadir of the human situation in time and place, sweeps on, and through, and beyond it. The resurrection is the sign of the victory of Christ over death; it is also the victory-sign flying over the entire history-involved assault of God upon man's sin and alienation. The man who is the Incarnation of God's will-to-restoration disappears in death and darkness—and then reappears. It was this reappearance that gathered faith about itself, created the community of believers called the Church, and drew up into its mighty meaning all the smaller and partial meanings that emerged in tentativeness during the days of his teaching.

The term shape, or morphology, is used to speak *both* of what God does in his action in Christ, and what this Christ-action accomplishes in the believer, for two reasons. First, to insure that the continuity between the once-done deed and its continuous working be clearly designated in language; and, second, to point to the large wholeness of the action—to liberate our comprehension of the scope, movement, and pattern of what God does in Christ from imprisonment in isolated episodes of the drama. There are facts, both in the biblical record, and in the history of its interpretation, which seduce the mind from the perception of this central pattern. So richly does the biblical literature speak of man's life and fortunes, miseries and delights, so panoramic is the scope of its utterances, so inwardly suggestive and fascinating its presentation of separate episodes, that the center of the multiform drama can be obscured. It is the chief utility of contemporary biblical studies that this fragmentation has been largely overcome, and the theocentric character of the literature brought again into focus. The story is about God! And no facet of it glows in its intended color unless it be placed under that primary source of light. God is the initiator of the basic and permeative thrust, God's will-to-restoration is the dynamic power in all movement, the implacable holy love of God brackets all accounts of man's nature, his career, and his destiny. Only this angle of vision can draw up into intelligibility and coherence the myriad episodes of the story.

A particularly sharp instance of this central force is the 139th Psalm. It is there confessed that no effort of man to know himself, find himself, be himself, is a viable possibility outside the God-relationship. God's knowledge of man is prior to man's knowledge of himself; and to know ourself to be known by God is asserted to be the precondition of all wisdom and all peace.

> O Lord, thou hast searched me and known me!
> Thou knowest when I sit down and when I rise up;
> thou discernest my thoughts from afar.
> (Ps. 139:1-2)

Flight from this prevenient knowledge leads through anxiety to frustration, to despair. Man's spirit has a three-dimensional possibility for escape—up, down, and out.

Whither shall I go from thy Spirit?
Or whither shall I flee from thy presence?
If I ascend to heaven, thou art there!
If I make my bed in Sheol, thou art there!
If I take the wings of the morning and dwell in the
    uttermost parts of the sea,
even there thy hand shall lead me,
    and thy right hand shall hold me. (Ps. 139:7-10)

Even the twilight of the subconscious and the night of the unconscious offers no obliterating anodyne.

If I say, "Let only darkness cover me,
    and the light about me be night,"
even the darkness is not dark to thee,
    the night is bright as the day;
    for darkness is as light with thee.
For thou didst form my inward parts,
    thou didst knit me together in my mother's
    womb . . .
Thou knowest me right well;
    my frame was not hidden from thee
when I was being made in secret
    intricately wrought in the depths of the earth.
                    (Ps. 139:11-15)

The same acknowledgment of an aggressive theocentric pattern, the same largeness of treatment, is necessary to indicate the accomplishment of this deed in history. If we ponder the way the early church declared the reality of its liberated and restored life in God we are immediately struck by an obviously non-accidental congruity between the shape of God's deed and the terms used to declare the shape of the restored life of the community. The abundance of dramatic terms, and the secondary employment of spiritual, moral, religious terms, in such declarations is astounding. " Do you not know that all of us who have been baptized into Jesus Christ were baptized into his death? We were buried therefore with him by baptism into death, so that as Christ was raised from the dead by the glory of the Father, we too might walk in newness of life. For if we have been united with him in a death like his, we shall certainly be united with him in a resurrection like his— so you also must consider yourselves dead to sin and alive to God in Christ Jesus."

In his letter to the community of believers at Philippi Paul unfolds with unparalleled clarity the re-enactment–dynamics of his life as " a man in Christ." With great boldness the Apostle transposes into terms descriptive of his own life the stark historical events of the life of his Lord—suffering, death, resurrection, a new life. " For his sake I have suffered the loss of all things, and count them as refuse, in order that I may gain Christ and be found in him, not having a righteousness of my own, based on law, but that which is through faith in Christ, the righteousness

35

from God that depends on faith; so that I may know him and the power of his resurrection, and may share his suffering, becoming like him in his death, that if possible I may attain the resurrection from the dead."

New Testament commentators, from Origen to the present, have been struck by the fact that the theological and ethical terms of Paul's speech are instant counterparts in the experience of *redemption* of the recorded cultural facts of the Synoptic record. This record is, by Paul, transposed into terms descriptive of new, operative vitalities in the life of the believer.[1]

Language like the foregoing, which is not singular but quite representative of the New Testament testimony of the new life of the community in Christ—such language is dramatic in the highest degree. The Christian life is here understood as a re-enactment from below on the part of men of the shape of the revelatory drama of God's holy will in Jesus Christ. The dynamics of this life are not abstractly indicated, nor is its creative power psychologically explicated. Suffering, death, burial, resurrection, a new life—these are actualities which plot out the arc of God's self-giving deed in Christ's descent and death and ascension; and precisely *this same shape of grace*, in its recapitulation within the life of the believer and the faithful community, is the nuclear matrix which grounds and unfolds as the Christian life.

36

The New Testament, to be sure, has abundant material which is immediately ethical: admonition, teaching, counsel, specific moral advice, minute directions for behavior in solitude and in the fellowship of the community. But the pastoral assumption back of all such teaching is precisely this continuity of the Christ-Life and the Christian life. Particularly illuminating is the situation to which St. Paul addresses himself in the Philippian letter. " So if there is any encouragement in Christ, any incentive of love, any participation in the Spirit—Have this mind among yourselves, which you have in Christ Jesus, who, though he was in the form of God, did not count equality with God a thing to be grasped—humbled himself and became obedient unto death . . . ."

This passage is a microcosm in which can be glimpsed the dynamics, the structure, and the sequence of Christian ethics. The Apostle feels impelled to address a concrete situation in the Philippian Christian community. No sooner, however, has he stated the problem and announced what pattern must prevail, than he buries the roots of the concrete requirement in nothing smaller than the mighty deed of God in Christ. Hence, the strange, " high christological " utterance occurring in the apostolic rejoinder to an earthy, disruptive demonstration of egocentricity. This passage gains in authority if, as Lohmeyer asserts, its represents Paul's recollection of a passage from the oral tradition very early fashioned by the vitalities of liturgical speech into these memorable rhythms. There is no need, as troubled but unimaginative commentators have sometimes caused themselves, to search extra-circumstantial sources for the original home of this resounding passage. The ripples of life's concrete decisions are continuous with the huge tidal wave of God's will in Christ; and any effort to articulate a Christian ethics apart from this enactment–re-enactment structure operates with ideas foreign to the New Testament.

During the months the substance of these pages was maturing and the category of shape more and more clearly emerging as the only operational idea adequate to New Testament discourse, there was being made available to English readers, in translation, Dietrich Bonhoeffer's essays on Christian ethics. From this work the following quotation is taken:

> . . . the Holy Scriptures speak of formation in a sense which is at first entirely unfamiliar to us. Their primary concern is not with the forming of a world by means of places and programs. Wherever they speak of forming they are concerned only with the one form which has overcome the world, the form of Jesus Christ. Formation can come only from this form. But here again it is not a question of applying directly to the world the teachings of Christ or what are referred to as

Christian principles, so that the world might be formed in accordance with these. On the contrary, formation comes only by being drawn in into the form of Jesus Christ. It comes only as formation in His likeness, as *conformation* with the unique form of him who was made man, was crucified, and rose again.[2]

In the history of Christian thought there is no one who has so fully explicated the Christian life as a new formation engendered by the Form of the deed of God in Christ as Irenaeus. The following, from his *The Demonstration of the Apostolic Preaching* is characteristic of his method. Irenaeus operates with a series of dramatic parallels by which he illustrates how the Incarnation in history overcomes man's moral defeat. The second Adam recovers the lost dominions of the first Adam; Mary, the second Eve, overcomes by her obedience the apostasy of the first Eve; the obedient second Adam in the garden of Gethsemane overcomes the disobedient first Adam in the garden of Eden, and so on.

And, because in the original formation of Adam all of us were tied and bound up with death through his disobedience, it was right that through the obedience of Him who was made man for us we should be released from death: and because death reigned over the flesh, it was right that through the flesh it should lose its force and

39

let man go free from its oppression. So the *Word was made flesh*, that, through that very flesh which sin had ruled and dominated, it should lose its force and be no longer in us. And therefore our Lord took that same original formation as (His) entry into flesh, so that He might draw near and contend on behalf of the fathers, and conquer by Adam that which by Adam had stricken us down.[3]

Fragments of this New Testament morphology (whereby the recapitulation-character of the Christian life is symbolized by the parallel structure of the biblical events) linger on in the liturgies of those churches which cherish continuity. The preface to the Holy Communion which is read during Lent is as follows: "Who on the Tree of the Cross didst give salvation unto mankind; that whence death arose, thence life also might rise again: and that he who by a Tree once overcame, might likewise by a Tree be overcome, through Christ our Lord; through whom with Angels etc. . . . ."

God does the redemptive and restorative deed; and God creates the response which is man's reception of it. So adequate are the God-initiated vitalities there deployed that Christian ethics is under no necessity to import into its basic structure anything at all from the rich and ennobling tradition of philosophical thought about the good, the valuable, and so on.

This is by no means to deny that philosophical ethical reflection has served by its work of analysis and the destruction of illusions, to sensitize men to the centrality and complexity of ethical problems. The continuing philosophical concern with the idea of natural law, inconclusive but persistent, is an instance of the fact that all efforts by man to know what he ought to do, drive him into trans-individual areas of his existence. Plato and Pascal have so illuminated the ambiguity of the moral personality as to place all men permanently in their debt. The truth they disclose may be submerged by arrogant pretensions or evaded by thoughtlessness, but when events revivify moral gravity this silenced truth erupts again to judge, illumine, humiliate into openness. The enormous literature of philosophical ethics is in this sense a profound and moving *confessional* which confirms the relevance of the radical drama of redemption which the Christian faith declares.

It is definitely not asserted here that the philosophical enterprise has no relevancy to the concrete tasks of Christian ethics; it is simply asserted that the faculty of reflection when functioning within the structure of the Christian ethical life must not betray that structure. The entire sequence from God's act, the re-enactment in the believer, the precise concrete duty of obedience in the tangled criss-cross of obligations that life presents—all of this is the old and ever

41

new realm of moral philosophy. But just as it is a proper task of philosophy to reflect upon the nature and meaning of man's enquiry about God without in that enquiry coming to the knowledge of God, so it is proper to philosophical ethics to insure that the ethical implications of man's incessant enquiry about God be not ignored.

If, as we have asserted, the *shape* of the deed of God and the shape of its response is dramatically presented in the Bible, it is possible with equal clarity to discern the *content* of God's work in the Christ-deed? This is, indeed, possible, but perception of it has been clouded by a prevailing disposition in Biblical interpretation. This disposition, characterized by the dominance in popular understanding of Jesus as essentially an exemplar of humane benevolence and spirituality, has for several decades now been brought under radical criticism and reconstruction in theological and biblical studies. These studies have had slight effect upon the temper of Christian thought in the ordinary American parish. As a result the ethical reconstruction which must inevitably follow upon the repudiation of a moralistic and religious-sentimental understanding of the Gospels has not been envisioned.

What is the content of the Christ-deed, which deed is to be understood as redemptive and restorative? If one consults the works on Christian ethics which are largely influential in this decade, one discovers that the reconstruction of the biblical portrait of Christ, which has been so powerful a feature of twentieth century Protestant thought, has simply not reached out and inwardly controlled our understanding of ethics. The strength of Christ which is primarily celebrated in these works, is love. At first sight this judgment seems unassailable, for surely He manifested the strength of love, demanded it of His disciples, and empowered them for its exercise.

The discernment of this strength of love has provided the motif for interpretations of the Christian life all the way from Adolf Harnack to Reinhold Niebuhr. Adolf Harnack declared that Jesus recognized love as the single root and motive, as the entire moral principle, of man's life.

> He knows no other, and love itself, whether it takes the form of love of one's neighbor or of one's enemy, or the love of the Samaritan, is of one kind only. It must completely fill the soul; it is what remains when the soul dies to itself.[4]

Reinhold Niebuhr, despite his distinguished participation in the recovery of biblical realism which is so notable an aspect of current Christian thought, is in fundamental agreement with Harnack. Central to his argument is the phrase, " The absolutism and perfectionism of Jesus' love ethic." [5]

43

We shall get a true answer to our question about the content of Jesus' deed only when we bring this entire tradition of " love ethic " under radical question. There are many terms which indicate the innermost fire in the person and work and demand of Jesus, and love, to be sure, is one of these. Others are faith, peace, joy, hope. Each of these terms is a function of what animates them all: his career is an utterly unique and monumental realization of a human life utterly determined by the God-relationship. One must stand in awe and openness before this fact—and interpret every term declarative of it as dragging the mind into its depth. Love, for instance, is never commanded for its own sake. It is not an absolute. God is the absolute One; and the strength of love is in the love of God and the love of the neighbor in God. The unity of Jesus' person is in the fulness of his own being in his God-relationship, his absolute relation to the Absolute. Both quantitative and qualitative analysis of the Gospels reveals no other constant and central power. Professor Richard Niebuhr says very justly:

> For Jesus there is no other finally love-worthy being, no other ultimate object of devotion, than God: He is the father; there is none good save God; He alone is to be thanked; His kingdom alone is to be sought. Hence the love of God in Jesus' character and teaching is not only compati-

44

ble with anger but can be a motive to it, as when He sees the Father's house made into a den of thieves, or the Father's children outraged. Hence, it is also right and possible to underscore the significance of this virtue in Jesus, while at the same time one recognizes that according to the synoptic Gospels, He emphasized in conduct and in teaching the virtues of faith in God and humility before Him much more than love.[6]

When in the Pauline literature we confront a vital working out of what the response to God actually was in the Christian community, we become aware that the re-enactment of the Christ-life from below is in fact a tremendous drama of *faith*. It is not possible to state too strongly that the life of the believer is for Paul the actual invasion of the total personality by the Christ-life. So pervasive and revolutionary is this displacement and bestowal that terms like influence, example, command, value, are utterly incapable of even suggesting its power and its vitally recreating force. The Apostle is therefore forced to create for this experienced work of God done in Christ and actualized in faith, a quite personal vocabulary. Efforts to explicate this life-in-Christ according to philosophical and psychological concepts deliver only a series of generalizations completely inadequate to the facts which inform and ring out of the man's words and works.

For me to live is Christ—if any one is in Christ, he is a new creation, the old has passed away, the new has come—it is no longer I who live, but Christ who lives in me, and the life I now live in the flesh I live by faith in the Son of God who loved me and gave himself for me—For you have died, and your life is hid with Christ in God.[7]

In St. Paul's faith-obedience, the commandment of love to God and love to neighbor *is transposed in terms of faith.* Faith, for Paul, is the comprehensive term used to designate the life-from-below which is the creation of the whole response of the deeds and the commands of God in Christ.

This transposition whereby love from above is received, interiorized, and actualized from below in terms of *faith*, has about it nothing arbitrary or accidental. For only faith is a large enough term to point to the total commitment of the whole person which is required by the character of the revelation. The very strangeness of the deed of a God who in concrete Incarnation in the earth-scene of man's death and lovelessness dies death out of its ancient dominion, and loves love into the supreme activity of God—this very strangeness evokes as adequate to itself nothing less than a totality response which is called faith.

When one seeks for the power of God in Christ he becomes aware that he stands before a quite new and astounding possibility for human life inwardly achieved, variously expounded, dramatically illustrated in the life of Jesus himself. Faith, love, obedience, joy, hope—these are not separate virtues, qualities, or exhibitions of the fire of the God-relationship for Jesus; they are, rather, the rich vocabulary of an organic oneness with the Father announcing and doing God's will in the living continuity of obedience.

It is only in the acknowledgment of this organic continuity that the words, works, commands of Jesus can be understood so as to supply the Church both with its elemental Christology and its ethical form, force, and style.

The development of western Christology along lines which subordinate the biblical strand known as the servant-Christology to another strand known as logos-Christology has made it difficult for western Christianity to pass organically from Christology to ethics. In recent works, in Christology and in general New Testament interpretation, this is being recognized. The patristic necessity to explicate the person and work of Christ in terms appropriate to the world of the west has powerfully overlaid the primitive Christian servant-Christology with layer after layer of ontological speculation; and the result has been to obscure the functional strand in the New Testament testimony to Christ. So strong has been the insistence upon the assertion that Christ does what he does because he is who he is, that inadequate attention has been paid to the testimony that he also is affirmed to be who he is because he does what he does.

The book of the Acts is here a primary source. In the Acts Jesus is proclaimed Christ and Lord in virtue of his work as obedient, utter accomplisher of the will of God. " So let all the house of Israel understand beyond a doubt that God has made him both Lord and Christ, this very Jesus whom you have crucified." (2:36) " The God of Abraham, the God of Jacob, the God of our fathers glorified Jesus his servant." (3:12) " It was for you that God raised up his servant." (3:26)

Christian ethics is *Christological* ethics, not in the sense that such ethics are correlates derived from propositions about Christ, but in the sense that they are faithful re-enactments of that life. In the Sermon on the Mount there is dramatized this obedient life in the bestowed and accepted love of God. The fulfillment and transformation of the entire Old Testament God-relationship is here clearly recorded. Here, as in every teaching, parable, miracle of Jesus, is disclosed a faith active in love which cracks all rabbinical patterns, transcends every statutory solidification of duty, breaks out of all systematic schematizations of the good—and out of the living, perceptive, restorative passion of faith enfolds in its embrace the fluctuant, incalculable, novel emergents of human life.

Concerning the persistent desire to set forth the meaning of Christian ethics in terms of the " principles of Jesus," two things must be said. In the first place, the methodology which works with principles subtly belies the very nature of the truth of Christianity. The truth of Christianity is neither abstract nor propositional; it is the truth of God incarnate in a person. " Grace and truth came by Jesus Christ "— " I am the way, the truth, and the life . . . ." Truth thus acted out and bestowed in historical existence is intrinsically incapable of transmission in terms of " principles." And in the second place, the desire to extrude principles from the Christ-life may be a form of man's hidden longing to cool into palpable ingots of duty the living stuff of love, and so dismiss ". . . the Holy One with whom we have to do . . . ."

The words of the Sermon on the Mount have been and remain an embarrassment to every effort to derive Christian ethics from Jesus according to principles of ethics. The style of speech in these words of Jesus is revelatory of the ground and the living activity of the ethics of faith. Professor Karl Heim has called our attention to the nonlegislative character of these utterances, which continue to fascinate the mind with system-disintegrating and disquieting power. These words do not constitute legislation replacing the old which, clearly put forth, can then be actualized by any devout and resolute person. The *occasional* character of these utterances is the clue to the non-legal, inexhaustible, principle-transcending intent and power of them. They are like lightning flashes of God's love-gift and command which, here and there, in this instance and now in that, flash over and brilliantly illuminate the moving sea below. Or, like a gull that flies smoothly over the turbulent sea and then suddenly in a quick, sure dart swoops down and picks up something out of the waters, resumes its flight and soars on.

These teachings of Jesus are not the legislation of love (the very term contradicts the nature of love) but are rather the paradigms of love. System is proper to the inorganic; the living has a characteristic *style*. Jesus in his teaching did not attempt a systematization or exhaustive coverage of all areas of human behavior. He did not, after the manner proper to philosophers of the good, attempt to articulate general principles which, once stated, have then only to be beaten out in corollaries applicable to the variety of human life. He speaks, rather, of God and of man and of the human community in a relational and a living fashion, and on the way, in the course of his speech swoops down, now here, now there; picks up some detail, situation, instance of human pathos, error, pride, holds it up for a moment, and then moves on.

This same uncalculated *style* is characteristic of the deeds of Jesus. His words and deeds belong together.

Both are signs which seek to fasten our attention upon the single vitality which was the ground and purpose of his life—his God-relationship. His parables, in this sense, are spoken miracles; his miracles are acted parables. His aphorisms are verbal apertures into his mission's meaning. In the fulfillment of this mission He proceeded through the countryside as a herald, judge, and teacher, but also as a healer and a helper. And His healing and His helping have the same gull-like, unanticipated immediacy as His tales. He confronted suffering, physical and mental torment, and regarded it as a characteristic mark of this world; only God's kingdom will show once more the finished creation, untouched by pain. Jesus' cures are not done in the course of a planned mission whose purpose was to cure the ills of as many sick persons as possible. If so, we should expect more of it, more teaching about healing, and a more systematic extension of it throughout the land.

We find nothing of the sort. Rather, the pattern is —*now here, now there*! This one He touches, others He does not. His cures do not signify an arbitrary anticipation of this kingdom, which no man knows when God will send. They indicate, rather, the present and pressing existence of the available power of the kingdom, now. They, too, are signs conveying the proclamation, the power, and the promise of the kingdom. They assert and demonstrate that the kingdom is on the way, that God, through the One whom he has sent is already permitting the splendor of the kingdom to shine out, now here, now there. Now, a certain centurion—now, by chance, a priest was going down that road—and behold, a man with a withered hand! The uncontrived, episodic nature of these happenings, the way in which each is made to glow in the reflected light and instance forth the power of God's pressing kingdom, is sufficient indication that they are sparks arching out from a central impact. The kingdom is the power; and these convulsive episodes are its transforming and revivifying works.

The *occasional* character of Jesus' words and works, which is asserted to be the point of entrance into the style of the obedient life, may appear to be so fragmentary and fugitive a pattern as to be useless for the requirements of present need and the urgent necessity to articulate a clear duty to the Christian community. This protest can so persuasively occur only because a persistent moralization of Jesus' deeds and commands has almost completely incapacitated men for immediate engagement with his living voice and work. A theological method more concerned with propositional coherence than with the description of historical reality and the communication of the personal vitality of Jesus has succeeded in making virtually inaccessible to Christian ethical discourse the actual facts of Jesus' own realization of the ethics of the God-relationship.

A second objection is, that insistence upon the peculiar style of Jesus' life, his repudiation of principles in favor of a vital pattern of response, may drive the question "What ought I to do?" so deeply down into the center of Jesus' own life as to destroy clarity by sheer depth, divert from present duties by the very glory of the New Testament portrait. This apprehension discloses a grave possibility, to be sure, and must be confronted. But the more clearly it is confronted, the more certain it is that for Christian ethics there is no other way. The risk belongs to the glory. The Good Samaritan stands there, and cannot be removed or forgotten by an ever-so-understandable desire that we might replace this thundering demonstration of the immediacy of obedient love by a clearer and less disquieting catalog of duties. Jesus not only told the story of the Samaritan, but added the absolue word that men ought to go out and do likewise. This command in the context of the story grips us, as Soren Kierkegaard says, "closer than a wrestler." And it is precisely within that grip that Jesus did act! He did intervene in the sphere of illness and suffering, and set Himself, now here, now there, against the structure and the course of this world. By these occasional lightning flashes and gull-like swoops into concrete situations, He released old captivities and opened up new possibilities for human lives. The kingdom of God " in your midst " was concretely certified by liberations, restoring deeds of love.

The absolute character of the ethical commands recorded in the Sermon on the Mount, and in other fragments in the New Testament, must be taken seriously. Critical studies of the Gospel record, which strongly suggest that it reflects here and there primitive Christian preaching fused with the words of Jesus, has multiplied the evidence that these sayings are the words of the Lord. Nor is it proper so to interpret St. Paul's words about the " overcoming " of the law in such a way as to efface or otherwise avoid coming to terms with these statements. The 13th chapter of I Corinthians is a Pauline confirmation of these ethical commands, not a " spiritual " substitute for them.

A clue to their interpretation is available if we assume that they are addressed to men as the terms of a parable are. They are aimed at the same form of cognition on the part of the hearer. They endlessly fascinate and trouble the mind and the conscience, spill out boundless creative power precisely because they inwardly resist all efforts to capture their vitality in systems of ethics.

These commands were uttered to men who, in all likelihood, were no better or worse than the rest of us. If these commands are not conceptually manageable they are not thereby unintelligible or nonsensical. The Speaker intended an explosive result—and nineteen hundred years have confirmed His success. As we ponder both the capacity of man to hear God speak, and the demonic capacity of man to settle for less than the mad obedience that God requires, the form of utterance in these commands will appear as the only conceivable way the Word of God to such men as we are could be conveyed. In support of that assertion the following propositions are submitted:

1. An absolute demand is the only verbal form by which to announce and release an *indeterminate* power, communicate an indeterminate promise, diagnose and judge man's indeterminate ability to deceive and excuse himself, enunciate an indeterminate possibility.

2. To be called to stand under the will of God as absolute demand is the only possibility by which to hold lives unconditionally responsible to God, the only way fully to celebrate the Godliness of God.

3. To have to live under the absolute demand is the only way, given man's power of dissimulation and self-deception, to keep life taut with need, open to God's power, under judgment by his justice, indeterminately dependent upon his love, forgiveness, and grace.

4. To have to stand under God's absolute de-

mand is the only way to keep man open to forms and occasions of obedience that the emerging and unpredictable facts of man's involvement in social change constantly present to him for his obedience. Even relative obedience, that is to say, can only sustain itself in the light of the absolute command.

5. Only the absolute demand can sensitize man to occasions for ethical work, and energize him toward even relative achievements. And only such a demand can deliver man, in these achievements, from complacency and pride; prevent him from making an identification of the justice of man and the justice of God.

6. Only the absolute demand has the transcendent freedom to stride forever out in front of all human accomplishments, fresh and powerful with the lure of deeper and more comprehensive goals.

7. The historical-relative requires the Godly-absolute even to see and to seek the better in the existing. Any understanding of the good without God will cease even to be good. Cut off from the absolute the relative ossifies into pride, becomes inert in the memory of past achievements, or makes a sardonic idol out of more and more smooth and profitable adjustments in the social order.

The kingdom of God is not a plan, or a program, or a concept, or an idea. It is a force within whose grip every man is caught; a grip never loosened, but rather having its ultimacy illustrated by every moral achievement and approximate obedience. It is a force, a godly fascination, and veritable *Imago Dei* engraved upon man's social history. The recollective fascination, once having flashed over and personally entered into history with its "signs" to which our Gospels bear witness, can never be forgotten. Its announcement and demonstration that the alienations of human existence in solitude and in society can be healed, and that the lost territory of life in God can be recaptured—this announcement and this demonstration, the root event of all Christian ethical thinking, guarantees that a holy possibility for human life will not cease to disturb, and here and there create new possibilities for it. Uncapturable in a concept, infuriating in its resistance to system, indestructible as a fact of power and a vision of promise, the realization of this life in men's lives is both the burden and the promise of Christian faith.

If the Christian ethical life is in reality the believers' re-enactment of God's action, then it is an absolute necessity of thought that the nature of this eternal drama of gift and response, as wholly determining the reactive ethical life, be clearly seen. It is here contended that such a perception is hindered when love is made the primary term for its designation. God, to be sure, is love; but it is not possible to pass from the love of God to what is required of men without causing our thoughts to pass through and come to terms with the *form* in which this love is revealed to men. The form of the revelation demands a transposition in the understanding whereby one understands that love revealed *in this particular form* begets a response, the proper name for which is *not love but faith*. In the Synoptic Gospels, in the Fourth Gospel, and in the letters of Paul, the vocabulary of response points to faith, not to love, as the generative center. Love, to be sure, is what faith does; it is the fulness and flower of faith. But this dare not blind us to the blunt fact that the " new being " of which the New Testament is the witness, is regularly designated *faith*. Peter at Caesarea-Philippi, the centurion whose son was healed, the woman in the house of Simon the Pharisee, the primacy of the term faith in Paul's exposition of the invasive progress of the Christ-life, the central role of faith in the Fourth Gospel's account of the career of Jesus—in all of these the role ascribed to faith is startlingly obvious.

The supreme revelation of God, who is love, is Jesus. But this Jesus as he appears to sense and sight is an historical fact. Neither to men of His own time and place, nor to men of any other time and place, does His appearance and career guarantee a revelation of God. When, for instance, a disciple exclaims who Jesus is and what is His ultimate meaning for human life, Jesus himself is quick to declare that " flesh and blood " (that is, the sum total of the humanly possible estimate) " have not revealed it unto thee, but my Father which is in heaven."

The historical form of a revelation of that which is neither born of man nor verifiable by history requires that nothing less than the decision of faith shall constitute the form of the response to it. That is to say, the love of God wherewith we are loved can become life in God wherewith we love only when this given-love bears forth its giving-love in the womb of faith.

God and faith belong together as the only possible correlation, given the form of God's revelation in an historical figure and deed. The structure of Christian theology—in which faith is the determinant in all things from the doctrine of God to the doctrine of the good, ethics—arises from this controlling fact: that all gifts from God to man are given in and pass through the historical; and the historical, *qua* historical, can never beget life, certainty, redemption. The historical form of God's redemptive deed compels the faithful form of man's response. No one in the history of Christian thought has seen this more deeply, or permitted it more utterly to determine his life and thought as a Christian, than Luther.

Faith is of things which do not appear. Therefore, that there may be room for faith, it is necessary that all things which are to be believed should be hidden. They cannot, however, be hidden more remotely than under their contrary object, sense, and experience. Thus, when God makes us alive he does it by killing us; when he justifies us he does it by making us guilty; when he carries us up to heaven he does it by leading us down to hell! [8]

Professor George Forell's volume, *Faith Active in Love*, gives a thorough explication and documentation of the relation of love and faith in Luther. The Reformer asks how love of the neighbor can be the fulfilling of the love when we are commanded to love *God* above all things, even above the neighbors! The answer, Luther declares, is given by Christ himself who said that the second Commandment is like unto the first, and Christ makes of love to God and love of one's neighbor an equal love:

And for this reason, first, that God does not need our work and kindness, but points us toward our neighbor that we may do for these what we may wish to do for him. He wants only that we trust Him and hold Him to be God. For even the preaching of His glory and our praising and thanking Him take place on earth so that our neighbor may be converted and brought to God thereby. And yet all this is called love to God,

—yet really to the use and profit of our neighbor only . . . . Here now a check is given to those slippery and skipping souls who seek God only in great and glorious things, who thirst after His greatness, who bore through heaven and think that they are serving and loving God by such noble ways, when all the time they are betraying Him and pass by Him in their neighbors here on earth in whom He desires to be loved and honored . . . . For therefore did He put from Him the form of God and put on the form of a servant, that He might draw our love for Him down and fasten it on our neighbors, whom we leave lying here, and gaze the while into heaven, thinking to show God great love and service.[9]

There are two reasons why this fundamental fact of biblically witnessed revelation has got to fight its way through to us who, within the tradition of the Reformers, might be expected to be more easily permeable to it. First is the fact that the situation in which Luther and the Reformers articulated the centrality of faith has tended to imprison the meaning of the term within the situation of the sixteenth century. When faith, that is to say, is understood exclusively in terms of an alternative to works, it is both reduced and intellectualized. It is reduced because it is imprisoned within the category of the individual relation to God and there effectually stifled, so that it may fail to exercise its creative power throughout the whole of the Christian ethical life. And, second, the assertion that the just shall live by *faith* means also that by faith the just shall *live!* The entire ethical dynamics of this affirmation is intellectualized when its vitality is transposed into theological propositions which are then believed adequately responded to if they win the mind's assent.

Both these tragic developments have characterized post-Reformation theology and have clouded the perception that a Christian can only live his life in virtue of the same gift in which he has his life. If a man is restored to God when he accepts what God gives (faith), then his restored life must be lived out in faith. If faith is the most comprehensive term for the God-relationship of the believer, then faith must be the comprehensive term for the life-relationship and activity of the believer. If a believer has a " new being " in faith in Christ, then his entire new " existence " is empowered by the same gift.

The believer is commanded to love, to be sure, but this love is formed in faith, just as the love of God who is in heaven is communicated in the faith-demanding historical deed of Jesus. The continuity of the love wherewith we are loved and the love which we are commanded to exercise, passes through the passion of faith. Only in this way can the relation of God's love for man and this loved-man's love for his fellow man be made clear and persuasive. For faith alone can rescue from nonsense the command to love. Nothing is more certain than that love cannot be commanded. If love, nevertheless, *is* commanded by Jesus, then some life-transforming new relationship in virtue of which the absurdity is overcome must exist. And precisely such a convulsive event in the God-relationship of men is the central declaration of the Gospel. "In this is love, not that we loved God, but that He loved us. . . ." Faith is here presented as a function of the love of God; it is a term descriptive of how man, now that God has taken the initiative, can be newly related to him. This biblical meaning of faith is totally obscured if the term is filled from below with materials taken from man's spiritual possibilities as these are historically manifested in man's general religious quest.

It was the experience of the holy particularity and the transforming power of this Godly love that inwardly shaped the literature of the New Testament. This love of God calls and draws men to its adoration and service. As the New Testament unfolds we see that faith is the name given that surrendering obedience-from-below which permits itself henceforth to have its life fashioned by this given love of God from above. The ultimate form of the giving, a death on the cross, is so contradictory and hidden a way for God to bestow his gift that faith alone is a response adequate to it. Love and faith are not, in the New Testament, alternative or opposing terms. Faith is the name for the new God-relationship whereby the will of God, who himself establishes the relationship, is made actual. And that will is love. Faith active in love is alone faith; and love is the function of faith horizontally just as prayer is the function of faith vertically.

The Content of the Engendered
Response

THE scope of a vitality is governed by its nature.
Boyle's law of gases asserts that a gas tends to
fill all available space. It is of the nature of the gospel
of redemption that all space, all personal relationships, all structures of society are the field of its
energy. The gospel of the Word of God made flesh
makes mankind the object of the gospel; the gospel in
the concrete figure of the man Jesus whose existence
was filled out within our mortal conditions—born of
a woman, betrayed, denied, crucified—makes the entire earthly life of every man the operational area of
this gospel. The gospel as redemptive event on the
field of history makes the configuration of historical
events the matrix of this gospel's working. The thrust
of the redemptive action of God is into the structure
of mankind, society, the family, and all economic
orders. The scope of that redemptive activity, restoring to God in faith and active in love, can clearly be
no more restricted than its originating action.

These clearly biblical facts stand in contradiction to
two dangers that have often crippled Christian expo-
sitions of ethics. The first is the practice of dividing
ethics into the categories of personal and social. Aside
from psychological and sociological facts which reveal

the severe limitations if not the actual absurdity of such a division, it is clearly not biblical in its understanding of God the Creator and man the creature. Man is created in community, and for community. The proverb " Ein Mensch ist kein Mensch " (A solitary man is no man) bluntly puts a truth which is central to biblical teaching. God's covenant is with a people; one of Jesus' most impassioned statements of his mission is in the word " gather "; and the obedience of primitive faith immediately understood its proper form in terms of a community of " the called " to " membership " in a " fellowship " which is " the household of faith " and which is " his body, the Church."

The second danger that operates to delimit the scope of the Christian life in its ethical vitality is one that has existed from the first days of the Christian era but confronts the believer today with peculiar power. It is the life-situation of millions of western men in their actual daily experience: the emergence and peril of the power-struggle between conflicting ideologies; the destruction, as a consequence of the technizing of material existence, of symbolic forms in which men traditionally have actualized their individuality and significance; the permeation of the realms of value, meaning, and all self-consciousness by the relentless momentum-to-bigness that characterizes the huge collectivities of politics, social life, the economic order. The stuff that men make meanings of can become so mechanized, rationalized, and "packaged," that the natural facts and processes of nature are concealed by the transformation of technology. While the workings of nature continue to exist and determine, they are rendered too febrile to support symbolic weight. A bottle of homogenized, pasteurized, and colorfully packaged milk may be safer for the body, but it contributes little to a child's empathy with the suggested Creator and Sustainer of "the cattle on a thousand hills." Our generation is just young enough to know with immediate comprehension and delight what Dylan Thomas is talking about in the first stanza of his *Fern Hill*:

> Now as I was young and easy under the apple boughs
> About the lilting house and happy as the grass was
>   green,
>   The night above the dingle starry,
>   Time let me hail and climb
>   Golden in the heyday of his eyes,
> And honoured among wagons I was prince of the
>   apple towns
> And once below a time I lordly had the trees and leaves
>   Trail with daisies and barley
>   Down the rivers of the windfall light.[1]

And we are old enough, and have lived long enough with apples packed in the State of Washington on

Monday and consumed in Illinois on Friday, to know what A. E. Housman's lad is living through when he says:

> Into my heart an air that kills
> From yon far country blows . . .
> What are those blue remembered hills,
> What spires, what farms are those? [2]

This life-situation can be described in such a way as virtually to identify it with the demonic and hence exhort men to withdraw from any engagement with the very forms of society within which they are placed. Such a course is both futile and wrong: futile because it flees the facts, and wrong because it tempts men to suppose that both the power of the divine redemption and the power of human creativity are restricted to venerated ways of ordering the human community. It is ironical that certain proponents of this position nostalgically assess as better than existing structures of community life circumstances which are historical memories precisely because they failed to meet the needs of millions of men! Accurate descriptions of contemporary life which point out its perils and corruptions, its thrust toward the " thingification " of man, are to be regarded as challenges to the scope and creativity of ethical life, and not as excuses for failure or devout rationalizations for lack of positive effort.

68

There is a strain in Protestant piety which makes it particularly susceptible to the temptation to interpret the counsel to keep oneself " unspotted from the world " in terms of quietism. The very historical matrix within which Protestant Christianity arose guarantees that the actual situation of the solitary individual before God should be insisted upon as the impact-point of the message of alienation, forgiveness, restoration. Insistence upon the inescapable responsibility of the individual has both prophetic power and peril. Its power is in its truth; its peril is in its tendency to make a false stopping point out of a true starting point, to force a definition of scope out of a point of impact, to restrict responsibility to the dimension within which that responsibility was learned.

The gospel itself is the corrective of all restrictive distortions of the gospel. The same gospel which demands intense inwardness as the theater of faith points to the world as a field of faith. The same Lord who meets, judges, heals, and forgives, in the solitary and naked aloneness of the self, plunges that self into the actuality of the world as its proper place for faithful activity in love.

The content of Christian ethics is disclosed in ever new and fresh ways as men's actual situations are confronted by God's revelation in Christ. When this assertion is taken seriously, certain old problems which have confused Christian ethical teaching are seen in a

new way. The will of God, for instance, declared
to be supremely revealed in Jesus Christ, cannot now
be identified with the Ten Commandments. The
Ten Commandments are now seen to be disclosures
of the Creator—creature structure of existence, of the
holy Source of all that is, of the requirements that
inhere in the human situation simply by virtue of
its source in God and the structure which he has
given it. Because God is Creator his reality is not to
be denied by idolatrous substitution of any earthly
source, good, value or purpose as ultimate. (I am the
Lord Thy God, thou shall have no other gods before
me.) Because God is the Creator the given structures
of dual sexuality, marriage, family, the reality and
needs of child-life are to be honored and protected.
(Honor thy father and thy mother. Thou shall not
commit adultery.) The integrity of personal life is
not to be violated. Because God is the Creator, men's
lives and those things which they fashion and use for
support and delight are to be respected. (Thou shall
not kill; thou shall not steal; thou shall not covet.)

The Ten Commandments, as the law of God, are a
verbalization of the given structures of creation. They
stand above all men, believers and non-believers alike,
as an accurate transcript of the facts—that the world
is of God, that ultimate relations among men and
things are grounded in him. The Stoic-immanental
concept of *natural law* with which many systems of

philosophical ethics operate is not introduced here because it is not needed. The perceptions and needs that require this concept are, in Christian ethics, completely confronted, and their space filled by the doctrine of God the Creator. The deed of God in Christ, however, occurred in a world which had and knew the Ten Commandments. If the deed is redemptive in intention and in fact, that does not deny or abrogate the revelation of God the Creator, but rather fulfills in the strategy of redemption what man regularly fractures in the structure of creation. Redemption does not destroy creation but realizes it. Grace does not destroy nature but fulfills it. This fulfilling and realization is generated in men who by faith in God's new beginning with them in the second Adam, Christ, are given what the New Testament calls a " new being."

This faith, this " new being " in Christ, is not only a restoration to fellowship with God in the forgiveness of sins, but an entirely new placement and activity in the midst of the world. Here and now in this living situation the believer is both forgiven and commanded. The forgiveness is of God's love, and the command is to actualize in history the same love which accepts, forgives, and restores the believer.

The content of this love is disclosed to the believer in his own obedience to it. " He that does the will shall know the truth." " If you love me you will keep my commandments." This does not mean that because the believer loves his Lord he has formal cause to keep the Lord's commandments; it means, rather, that the commandment and the actualization of the love of Christ are in organic continuity. To love is to serve; and to love Christ is to serve him where he presents himself in his identification with needy men for our service.

What then is the specific content of this faith-active-in-love at the point where Christ meets us in man? The moment the question is put that way (which is the way the New Testament puts it) we comprehend what is meant by the assertion that Christian ethics discloses its content at the point of God's revelation of himself in Christ. Only now are we ready for that concentration of content which confronts us in such a passage as Matthew 25:31-46. In this teaching Jesus presents himself for the service of faithful love in absolute identification with human need—loneliness, estrangement, hunger, thirst. There faith sees him, there faith must obey him.

Christian ethics is the actualization of justification. For justification, being certified or made righteous in the God-relationship, bestows positive liberation to serve. This liberation exists inwardly because, as Luther puts it, " God has taken care of my salvation in Christ," and I am henceforth free as before God. This liberation exists outwardly because the energies which men futilely devote to the pleasing of God are now called out and exercised where God's purposes and family require them. When the self is known, loved, forgiven, then the self is set free in disciplined service to the will of God. And this will of God is now confronted both as a known and as an unknown. It is known in Christ who is the incarnate concretion of God's ultimate and relentless will-to-restoration; and it remains unknown in the fact that the actual service of this will is presented to the believer not as a general program given in advance but as an ever-changing and fluctuant obligation to the neighbor in the midst of history's life.

Corollary to this known (which is the love of God as giver and restorer) and corollary to the unknown (which is the precise form the love of the neighbor requires in novel situations) is what Alexander Miller has called " An absolute element and an element of calculation." He comments, " But Christian ethics differs from idealist ethics in that its absolute is an absolute loyalty and not an absolute principle. While the Christian calculation differs from typical pragmatism in that while there is always a hidden absolute in pragmatism, an unadmitted presupposition about what is good for man, in the Christian scheme the calculation is grounded in a very precise understanding of what is good for man, determined by the revelation of God in Christ: ' Live life, then,' says St.

Paul, ' not as men who do not know the meaning and purpose of life, but as those who do.' " [3]

It is now possible to speak somewhat more specifically of the dynamics of Christian ethical decision and to indicate how these operate. If not by appeal to principles, or in patternless dependency upon the mercurial stuff of one's chance observations and occasionally animated affections—then what alternative remains?

Christian ethical decision is generated between the two poles of faith and the facts of life. Each of these acts upon the other: facts act upon faith to reveal to it the forms available as its field of action; faith acts upon facts to discover their meaning and peril and promise for men.

Facts without faith are blind; faith without facts is empty. Facts are never *mere* facts. They are what they are plus an indeterminate, undetermined potential. And one aspect of faith is certainly this, that it bestows upon its child sensitiveness to dimensions of possibility that are not otherwise discerned. Faith does not diminish the facticity of facts; but faith enlarges and penetrates the world of fact with its peculiar livingness. The quality of this creativity, Christianly known, is not disclosed when its source is sought in man's natural vitalities, or in the reason's power whereby old stasis is made malleable to the mind's vision; but ultimately it is found in the power of

that love which " so loved the world " that it endlessly creates new fields for its realization in history.

The confused and often contradictory nature of
the facts with which we are confronted presses obedience down to the operational level of faith. Faith
interprets facts in terms of their specifically human
content. That is why the facts of human misery in
post-war Europe discovered to millions of Christians
in prosperous America a contemporary field for the
operation of their faith; and faith penetrated these
facts with its unique dimension, revealing in this
anguish not only men needing coats and calories, but
human beings whose lives could be restored to meaning by nothing less than personal identification with
them in their hurt by fellow children of the crucified
object of the common faith. It is precisely the salvatory power of this uniquely faithful deed of love,
whose content included the ancient word and the
sacraments, which was not understood by those who
would adequately treat all crucifixions with calories.

This means that the will to help must devise the
means to help in ways determined by the actual collectivities within which men are deepeningly involved, and within which interdependency each man
is related to all men by a thousand cords. Needs that
are shaped by structures must be met by help that
also is structured! The requirement of justice is not
only not ignored by Christian ethics, but is in an even

more urgent sense an actually effective way to bring the help of the group-concern to bear upon the needs which are created, in part, by the group way of life.

That faith should seek to realize its proper obedience in alliance with the struggle for and the use of the instruments of justice does not by any means constitute a distortion of the gift and primacy of faithful ethics; it is, rather, faith's realistic acceptance of the root-fact of collective life—that the quest for justice is a drive built into all human relationships. It is there, not primarily as an ideal envisioned by human reflection, but as a vision engendered by a dimension of man's self as a creation of the Creator.

There are, indeed, needs of the neighbor, uninvolved with patterns of group life; these confront the believer with a demand for concern which is immediate, simple, urgent. But deepening areas of contemporary man's need are shaped by and involved with his existence in the huge collectives of economy, politics, community organization. Love must grasp the kind of hand that need holds out. The quest for justice is, on the one hand, an effort to understand the peculiar requirements of human life in its mobile career, and, on the other hand, to create instruments of positive law to certify these requirements, set limits to forces that would ignore them, and order collective life toward a tolerable balance of goods.

This means that love and justice are not two forms of the obedience of faith; they are modes of life's responsibility for lives. The apparently impersonal arrangements which justice makes to serve a need may cover the face of the need with pipes, valves, and pumps. But the need, the stuff, and the arrangements are not thereby bereft of the holiness that all faithful obedience has. A cup of cold water for my neighbor's need can no longer be actualized by simply sensitizing mercy or multiplying cups. The town pump for a few dozen has been displaced by a gigantic water supply system for millions; and concern that justice should prevail in the procurement, distribution, availability, and price of water is the hard, pragmatic face that love wears. And justice and technical competence are the hands it must work with. Justice is not identical with love; and the potencies and ingenuities of love are not exhausted in the struggle for justice. But justice is a primary instrument of love and a field for its operation. This has always been so, as the prophets of Israel so passionately insisted; it is so now and with a heightened urgency.

Just as it is necessary to relate faith-active-in-love and the quest for justice, so it is necessary at the same time to assert that this relationship is not an identity. For while the God-relationship, which is both source and content of faith and love, acknowledges the requirements of justice as also from God, the nobility of the quest for justice can exist and trouble men's lives without such a recognition. Justice can exist without any acknowledgment of the God-relationship; but the God-relationship cannot exist without concern for justice.

A comparison of the terms *justice* and *righteousness* will clarify the point. Justice is a term whose referent is an ideal balance of goods, duties, satisfactions within the human community. This ideal, and some effort to realize it, is not foreign to any culture whose story is available to us. To account for the existence of the ideal of justice it has not been necessary to postulate a divine source. Vitalities operative within empirical society have been powerfully generative of the quest for and the creation of various structures of justice. With such accounts the Christian understanding of the Creator cannot be satisfied; and in its doctrine of God the Creator and Redeemer, it has insisted upon relating justice to the creative and restorative will of God.

But the biblical term *righteousness* is grounded precisely in a postulate that justice need not propose. Righteousness is a term used to designate human life sprung from, determined by, and accountable to the life of God. It is a thoroughly theonomous term. That is why, although faith-active-in-love ought to relate itself to all in human life which seeks justice,

78

this faith can never account for itself nor be at rest with the achievements of justice.

If, then, faith is to be active in love, and if justice in the huge and impersonal collectivities of contemporary life is love operating at a distance, how are the energies of love to be related to that practical ordering of life in community which is called politics? Preliminary to any effort to speak to this question must be a comment about the term politics. The term indicates that nexus of practical arrangements for the creation of order, the enhancement of community values, the protection of life, and the provision of necessary services that every community is absolutely required to bring into existence under one form of government or another. The tradition in Christianity whereby this function is held to be "ordained of God" is thoroughly biblical; and the frequent lamentations of the pious over the dirt in politics may constitute but a devout mechanism whereby one avoids coming to terms with the problem at all. While most Christians today, to be sure, would admit that the Gospel is relevant to the realm of politics, they turn in revulsion from the actual operation of political parties and the devious devices required for the formation of practical policies. To involve themselves in jockeying, trading, calculation, compromise, baby kissing, and boodle-splitting requires a rough handling of ethical "principles." And in avoiding this danger they successfully avoid any contribution to public order. This attitude makes a certain sense if Christianity and the duties of the Christian man are identified with loyalty to a set of principles; but such an identification is both a reduction and a perversion of the Christian faith.

The state may sometimes make pretensions beyond the finite and mortal end and function for which it is ordained; and these pretensions are in continuity with that general disposition to idolatry which tempts men always and everywhere. Nevertheless, the state, ordained of God for limited and finite ends, is the necessary means by which the will to the good becomes effective for the correction of collective injustice and the restraint of inordinate greed. Luther's view of the state, in so far as it was tied to the peculiar political situation of his time, ought no longer be used as an adequate guide in our engagement with present problems. But he had an understanding of the function of state as a " mask of God " which far transcends his practical conclusions from princely-state circumstances of the sixteenth century, and is intrinsically more inclusive of the facts of human evil and political creativity than the state-view of either Geneva or Rome. For his call to men everywhere and in every circumstance to realize their vocation as the faithful service of God in daily work, shattered the false separation of sacred and secular, recognized the duties of the common life as valid structures for Godly service, and celebrated the entire creation as a field in which every believer is summoned to be a " little Christ " to his neighbor's need.

In this situation, in politics as in every other sphere, Christian ethics is given its content as it makes pragmatic selections among available alternatives to enhance and serve the common good, approximates ever more sensitively the demands of justice, and finds methods to allay tensions and curb inordinate desires. In this faithful process (which is the mortally ultimate situation!) the believer never transcends the fact that he is *simul justus et peccator* (simultaneously justified man and sinner). This is to say that ethical decisions are never delivered from, and ethical achievements never add up to, a position elevated above faith's obedient placement within, and joyful acceptance of, man's creaturely situation. Just as no achievement can place a man beyond the daily need of God's judgment, grace, and forgiveness, so that no ethical decision is ever wholly true, just, or good—so, also, men's efforts will forever stand under both the thrust and the limitation of the same situation. A particularly poignant illustration of this necessity confronts us as we consider efforts presently being made toward some kind of precarious peace among the nations. Here is the dilemma: because history—in this, like human life in general—can never wholly redeem, redress, cancel out, or compensate for past wrongs, the very efforts for present and future peace constitute a kind of " betrayal " of millions of men who are dead by the power of the evil, whose countrymen's torments remain, and whose loss of freedom may be permanent. But the present facts are of such a nature that the attempt to right what has been wrong would seemingly involve two vaster terrors: a struggle more full of pain and death than the one whose effects the nations seek to redress, and world-wide acceptance of the fateful use of now available weapons which might well obliterate the very possibility of anything resembling normal human life and freedom for the entire planet. But in the very moment one so concludes, he is aware that this apparently " Christian," rational, humane concern represents also a pious façade back of which lurks a hope not to disturb prosperity, the securities of one's own career and family. It is in part a kind of highly commendable " long view " which permits one to have his ethical cake and eat it, too!

The heartbreaking choices which confront us so sharply in the affairs of nations are but the transcript of the situation which is structural in the solitary life of the believing individual. In a recent book, *The Cruel Sea*, a dramatic instance of this is presented. The commander of a destroyer, convoying a fleet of merchant ships, has finally located the submarine

which had sunk several ships and caused the loss of
hundreds of lives. The sonar-device which located
the hidden submarine indicated that it was precisely
at the point where, on the surface of the water, some
hundreds of men, previously torpedoed, were swimming about. To drop a depth bomb for the destruction of the submarine would at the same time mean
the destruction of the men swimming in the water.
There was but an instant to make his choice, and the
commander made it knowing that no choice available
could be anything but death-dealing. The subsequent tormented statement of the commander, "One
must do what one must do—and say one's prayers,"
is an eloquent condensation of the ethical situation.
"One must *do*"—for inactivity, refusal to do anything, is already to do something. And that something is not good. ". . . what one *must* do" is not
an open choice; definite alternatives are absolutely
given. Both are deadly. ". . . and say one's prayers"
is an acknowledgment of deepest piety that no decision fulfills the will of God or releases man from
that relation to God which dares to live only by the
daily forgiveness of sins.

When the God-relationship is centrally informed
by faith, then the actual situation of decision-pressed
man is saved from the despair which would inevitably
overtake him if this relationship were simply compounded of love. For love, no matter how deeply

83

accepted from God, obediently directed toward men, firmly held to as the motivation of action, both reveals and compels the acceptance of pragmatic choices, *all* possible variations of which are fraught with inadequacy, pain, and denial. In this sense love is the tutor of faith! Even the " law of love," no less than the law of Moses, is a schoolmaster who leads the believer to Christ. For, in Christ, the believing lover of men-in-Christ now stands with his Lord and supreme Lover precisely in his crucifixion! " I am crucified with Christ " is a term expressive not only of the Christian recapitulation of the Christ-life in the large, but a symbol of the inner content of numberless ethical decisions in their actual heartbreaking character. A Christian ethics must, therefore, work where love reveals need. It must do this work in faith which comes from God and not as accumulating achievements to present to God. In this working it must seek limited objectives without apology, and support failure without despair. It can accept ambiguity without lassitude, and seek justice without identifying justice and love.

Ours is a generation upon which two forces from opposite directions are beating with such fury that we are in danger of ethical paralysis between them. From the one side we are the heirs of an ethical analysis which properly insists upon the will of God as transcendent to the relativity of all cultural life, reveals

84

the ambiguity of everything human, the admixture of self-interest in everything human, the lurking demonic in every positive course. The result of this penetrating effort to speak the truth about man as sinner in his modern situation has been that decisiveness before gigantic evils and shrieking human injustices has been paralyzed by the sheer fullness with which every man's evil has been revealed, and ethical complexity has been so elaborately analyzed as to stun the conscience.

From the other side, we are a generation before whose eyes every primal meaning of " The grace of the Lord Jesus Christ, the love of God, and the communion of the Holy Ghost " has been blasted by spirits organized into effective powers and threatening to reshape all existence into a one-dimensional denial of that God-relationship which constitutes humanity. Between these two forces—an analysis which reveals involvement and humble arrogance, and the fact of millions of men enslaved, betrayed, liquidated —the Christian believer is tempted to stand in horrified but inert repentance.

The repentance must remain, for it is the constant heartbeat of the man of faith in history; but the stasis must be overcome. We are sinners, to be sure, but precisely such sinners as are addressed by the word of St. John, that if a man see his brother in need and shut up his bowels of compassion, how dwelleth the love of God in him? Unless we can discover a way, both to acknowledge the facts, act in faith and love, and accept the consequences of our action, our generation will constitute a huge portrait of repentant believers with furrowed brows and inert hands.

The way of advance is to understand that it is a function of faith itself to discern the differences between facts and then act upon what it discerns. Faith without discrimination between facts is a sentiment that encourages brutality; faith without acts (works!) is dead. There is, to be sure, no human fact in which sin is not involved. But within some structures of fact there are alive, free, and operative forces of grace, insights of elemental justice, recreating energies of love. In politics, as in theology, freedom is a precondition of regeneration. It is a fact that the Negro community in American life has been exploited, contemptuously handled, overtly insulted by public law. It is also a fact that within American public life concerned men and institutions have been free to combat injustice, illumine ignorance, plead and work for equality of treatment.

The body of fact presented, for instance, by the Soviet reading of history and man, is a body of fact of a quite different order. It is a legitimate and necessary function of faith to discern this difference. For this closed matrix of dogma and force permits no operational space for the very forces which alone could corrode its idolatry, disintegrate its monodi-mensional dogma about man and history, and force it open to the powers of grace, justice, and love.

We began with the assertion that to be a Christian is to accept what God gives. We end with a reitera-tion of that assertion now so elaborated, it is hoped, as to disclose how the structure of Christian ethics grows organically out of the fact and the content of the endlessly giving God. The Christian man is to accept what God gives as Creator: the world with its needs, problems, possibilities; its given orders of fami-ly, community, state, economy. Each of these is invested with the promise and potency of grace, and each of these is malleable to the perverse purposes of evil.

The Christian is to accept what God gives as Redeemer: the earth and all human life as the place where God's glory became flesh and dwelt among us, and, therefore, the holy place for life in forgiveness, in the obedience of faith, in the works of love. " Man becomes man because God became man." God has given the form of himself and his will in a man; and the ethical life is the birth-pangs attending the new-being of man in history, ". . . until Christ be formed in you."

The Christian is to accept what God gives as Holy Spirit the Sanctifier. This acceptance includes the gifts that God gives from above; and the tasks which he gives in the world around. This gift and these tasks belong together. The gift is celebrated in the doing of the tasks; the tasks are undertaken in faith as witnesses to the gift.

NOTES TO THE TEXT

CHAPTER I

[1] *The Decline of the West: Perspectives of World History,* authorized translation with notes by Charles Francis Atkinson (New York: Alfred A. Knopf), II, 189.

[2] *The Collected Poetry of W. H. Auden* (New York: Random House, 1945), 145-46.

CHAPTER II

[1] See, for example, James S. Stewart, *A Man in Christ* (New York: Harper & Brothers, n. d.); and, Charles H. Dodd, *The Meaning of Paul for Today* (New York: George H. Doran Company, 1920); and Anders Nygren, *Commentary on Romans* (Philadelphia: Muhlenberg Press, 1949).

[2] *Ethics* (New York: Macmillan Company, 1955), 18.

[3] *The Demonstration of the Apostolic Preaching,* trans. from the Armenian by J. A. Robinson ("Translations of Christian Literature," Series IV, *Oriental Texts* [New York: Macmillan Company, 1920]), 21 ff.

[4] *What is Christianity?* (New York: G. P. Putnam's Sons, 1901), 78 f.

[5] *An Interpretation of Christian Ethics* (New York: Harper and Brothers, 1935), 39. This work is cited because its argument is that phase of Niebuhr's thought which is best known and most influential. It would be quite unjust, however, not to call attention to the deepening criticism and correction of this simple "love ethic" in Niebuhr's later work. In his book *The Self and the Dramas of History* (New York: Charles Scribner's Sons, 1955) is clear evidence of Niebuhr's supplanting of *love* by *faith* as the fulcrum in his continuing argument; and in Vol. II of the *Library of Living Theology,* edited by Charles W. Kegley and Robert W. Bretall (New York: Macmillan Company, 1956), there are several essays which question his earlier agreement with Harnack, and acknowledge the maturer Christianity of his later and current writings.

[6] *Christ and Culture* (New York: Harper and Brothers, 1951), 16. Professor Niebuhr's use of the term "virtue" in this work

89

would lead to confusion were it not clearly apparent in the entire discussion that the word is used in its original meaning of *strength*, and is devoid of the content common to its use in the older philosophical ethics.

[7] Cf. Phil. 1:21, II Cor. 5:17, Gal. 2:20, and Col. 3:3.

[8] Weimar edition, 18:633.

[9] *Faith Active in Love: An Investigation of Principles Underlying Luther's Social Ethics* (New York: American Press, 1954).

Chapter III

[1] *The Collected Poems of Dylan Thomas* (New York: New Directions, 1953), 175-80.

[2] *A Shropshire Lad* (New York: Shakespeare House, 1951), 62.

[3] Alexander Miller, *The Renewal of Man* (New York: Doubleday & Company, Inc., 1955), 44.